"HEART OF GRACE"

MY JOURNEY THROUGH ART AND ADVERSITY

CAROL CISNEROS

About the Author

Carol Cisneros, M.M., was born on September 29, 1951, in Chicopee Falls, Massachusetts. She attended St. Theresa's Academy in San Antonio, Texas, graduating in 1969. Carol furthered her education at Our Lady of the Lake University (1969-1970) and The University of Texas at San Antonio (1975-1978). She later earned a Bachelor of Arts and a Master of Music from Texas State University in San Marcos, Texas (BA, 1991; MM, 1995-1997).

ACKNOWLEDGEMENT

Alice Canestrsro "Pájara"

James T Fort M.M.

What would I do with out him? It's funny, but when I first met J.Ay I had completely wrote off any kind of romance relationship with another guy. Then he came along. We met on a gig, a New Year's Eve cake. Good money. With his long curly hair. His thick glasses and white Tennis shoes. I sit in myself, "Don't look at him." We've been inseparable ever since. 🤗

TABLE OF CONTENTS

CHILDREN DO DREAM

"When I was a little girl, my first wish

and ambition was to be a composer and singer. I believe I was only
10 years old and in the fourth grade. We were living in Tacoma,
Washington. I remember that our school took us to hear

Benjamin Britten,

the "Young Person's Guide to the Orchestra."

At the time, I was in the 4th grade studying violin,

my first real instrument.

Inspired by the composer Benjamin Britten

I knew then that I wanted to become a composer.

I was a dreamer then, even at the age of ten.

Children do Dream.

My neighbors across the street from us

took me to see "Porgy & Bess."

I spent the summer singing George Gershwin's "Summertime"

to anyone who would listen.

I was a dreamer then, even at the age of ten.

Children do dream

My step-grandfather also bought me the Smithsonian magazine for children, anything to do with nature, math, art, and learning. I only knew him as "Fadee'." I think he was Scott-English, and if I remember correctly, I think his last name was "Chapman." He was amazing, he loved me as I loved him. We spent a lot of time in the Garden, where he taught me so much about gardening. One morning, we watched the Morning Glories open and the vines that grabbed on to the fence and wooden sticks. I would collect eggs from the chicken coup while he would monitor the trap that collected doves, and they were delicious.

I began singing at sixteen at the downtown Methodist Church, across from the St. Anthony's Hotel on St Mary's Street. An upstairs coffee shop every Saturday night. Later, at the" Hilton Palacio del Rio," San Antonio Riverwalk, and the San Antonio World's Fair, "La Maison' Blanche," a French Restaurant where I sang outside. I would challenge myself to get as many customers walking by and persuade them to come inside the outside patio. They also fed me the most incredible delicious French food and pastries.

I spent most of my time singing with the Central Catholic High School Glee Club and "His Brother's Children." Central Catholic High School allowed the girls from all the female parochial Catholic High Schools to join their Glee Club. St Theresa's Academy was a very small school. It was run by the Theresian Nuns from France and England. My graduating class was only made up of twelve of my fellow students. My sister joined the Central Catholic High School Glee Club, and I'm thankful that my dad and mom made me join. It is there that I learned to sing and play guitar. My guitar teacher was Jesse Hernandez, a remarkable guitarist and friend.

The San Antonio Riverwalk was home throughout high school. I was one of the original "San Antonio River Rats." I think I must have performed every day and night for four years plus and loved every minute. At that age I knew what I wanted to do with my life, and that was to "sing," just "sing." And to sing with other musicians, we would have jammed all night if we could have.

Practicing was never a chore. I couldn't get enough of my guitar as I put my head on the side and listened to the notes and chords resonate. Sometimes, my father would yell at me to come in and go to sleep; after supper time, I would go outside and sit on the back porch and play my guitar. By then, it was two o'clock in the morning. Music was my consolation, my reassurance, and solace from the rest of the world.

I spent the fall and spring semesters at Our Lady of the Lake University.

I will always cherish the nuns; they gave me so many life skills, and I am eternally grateful.

SOMEONE ASKED, "WHY?"

Someone asked me, "Why am I an artist, a singer? Why, a musician, writer, poet, etc.? "Why don't you get a real job?" I am eternally grateful for the bounty the universe has given me. To be able to express myself both as an artist and a musician. Artistic expression pulls me towards my deepest passions. Like a star illuminating the night, it speaks softly, calling my name, and I listen in awe and wonder. Questioning myself, "Am I just created for the fusion of two hearts to become one." Which is good and well. Is that all there is? Can't I allow myself to be passionate about what I do? And I must admit, even though I am disabled and live with chronic pain, concerning my life as an artist and musician, I must admit that "I love it."

Creating and allowing this synergy, this Chi (the 22nd star in a constellation * the circulating life force whose existence and properties are the basis of much Chinese philosophy, medicine, balancing the body's flow "qui'...air, breath') overview (Google Dictionary Oxford languages) This electricity, quarks of gravitational pull, take me to places of intrigue and mysteries. This sacred energy, like the Holiest of Spirits, sustains me, letting creativity guide me through life's winding paths.

I have a need—a deep passion—to create expressions of life, ideas, and ideals of this Earth, this spiritual journey. I channel movement through the physical, the macro, and the metaphysical: balance, rhythm, and connections. These connections pull me closer to the things I love. I am implored by the earth's axis and its sister: the sky, the rivers, streams, creeks, oceans; its grandfather, the moon; grandmother, the forest, its mother: the earth, its brother, the stars and father: the sun; this glorious sun.

My notes on some elements of the world of art, music, and literature: Form: Everything has form, literature, music, art, and even our bodies. The three factors of form: the background, middle ground, and the foreground. Even when there appears to be two dimensions, considering art, there are actually several layers. And as we peel back each layer we begin to see something different each time.

Balance: Relationships don't have to be symmetrical to have balance. Polarity can include rhythm movement, like a ballet, where line, space, texture, and rhythm are created. And so the dance begins.

Color: the physical sense portraying the concrete as well as the abstract affection of the innermost, subjective, objective emotions. Bringing to mind "Ondas" (Spanish) and worlds of other realities of color. Where opposites attract, cool with hot complementing each other. For example, Red with green, yellow with violet, orange with blue, and so on.

The Quantum Entanglement: "a phenomenon in quantum physics that occurs when two or more particles (colors) become connected in such a way that the state of one particle can't be described independently of the other particles." "There is instant communication between particles." Einstein describes quantum entanglement as a "spooky action at a distance." Google AI Overview+-*

Rhythm: rhythm is another dimension of the art and the music world. The sound of a train skating across the railroad tracks, traffic soaring through a busy intersection. Rain that drips down my window pane.

My desire as a Mexican American Woman is to create more music, more art, more poems, literature, printmaking, more jazz, more creativity, more love, and continue the dance of love.

"Do you know how much I love you? Do you know how much I care. How much you mean to me. You are like the roses and the Marigolds, the Poppies in a sunlit field. The Begonias blooming in my garden. Red Sunflowers softly growing in my head. Even the Prickly Pears how lovely they are. How lovely the Hibiscus in your hair, and then suddenly I realize, (pause)

How lovely is the color red."

@ 21st Century Clausula

The inner tones of my heart so reminisce
Sounds of a substitute clausula ...
From plainchant into the vortex of jazz
Shades of emotion, conceptualize jazz
With each key signature having different
Shades of emotion... In other words
Not playing chord changes, but, playing concepts.
Now we begin to groove— Now we ...
Begin to grow ... a 21st century clausula.
©2023

"They tell me not to wear my heart on my shoulders, but it keeps showing up at the most inopportune times."

Woman Holding the Sun

Acrylic & Collage

WOMEN HOLDING THE SUN

"Could it be a dream? A sputnik satellite soaring above us, 'round and 'round in our mind's eye, and the crocodile and the serpent dance to the music of life, and she, yes, she holds creativity and key to life, the sun."

Beautiful Butterfly and the Planets

Mixed Media

Gold Spray Paint Collage and Acrylic Paint

BEAUTIFUL BUTTERFLY
AND THE PLANETS

"I love to watch nature, especially butterflies. This one caught my eye, and I thought to myself, how beautiful are God's creations. Butterflies are important. They are the epitome of freedom. They fly with fearless courage; butterflies are timeless. They are innocent and delicate but resilient. They are free from the hassles of life we bear every day. And they are free to love."

Dove and the Little Blue Bird

Mixed Media

Green and Blue Spray Paint on Torn Paper,

Acrylic Paint & Collage

DOVE AND THE LITTLE BLUE BIRD

"Dove and the Little Blue Bird, just like jazz, some things are not evident right away. As we uncover the layers of abstraction, we are able to see the Blue Bird and the Dove. Fragile but resistant to all that is dark and ugly. They represent the delicate balance of nature. The Dove has no gall bladder, no gall, no insolence, no audacity, no impudence. That is why the Holy Spirit is represented by a dove, "Purity of heart." The little Blue Bird is finding his way home; he is vulnerable, fragile, finding peace, strength, and happiness next to his friend, the Dove."

Birds

A Parakeet, Hummingbird & a Pelican

acrylic

WHAT THE UNIVERSE GAVE TO ME

What the Universe gave to me
The most beautiful mosaic from a mocking bird did sing.
It appeared to be 1,001 melodies
Variations of the sweetest perennial theme
One after another, did this songbird sing
And Oh, how she did sing, how she did love
How she did dream of these 1001 melodies.
A symphonic vision, stirring powerful imagery
Soulful, haunting, winsome, a variegated suite
Sweet and alluring treasured motif
And as I pondered this elegant pastiche
These elaborate and poignant images and harmonies
this variation of life's sweetest, beautifully dark
And wondrous poetry
How life did seem
An engaging lietmotif
What the universe gave to me
1001 melodies from a mocking bird did sing
Of untainted and cherished aspirations
A narrative of a lover's dream
Stirring powerful imagery
Of life's treasured symphony.

Red Violins

"Before I knew about scanners

I drew the violins with the mouse."

Computer Graphic design

ANOTHER THOUGHT OF THE DAY

Is my life just a dream?

Maybe a video stream

Sublime innovation

Control from an accidental

Twist of fate

Again,

Is my life just a dream

Maybe a video stream

Sublime innovation

Control from within

A twist of fate

Here, here

A toast to humanity

A toast to reality

A short-term hallucination

A processed memory

Maybe it's what I believe

Could this really be real?

Or just another String Theory reality?

Green Violins

Computer Graphic Design

I SHOULD BE WRITING

I should be writing

There's so much to say

A myriad of thoughts to portray

Thoughts of gaiety

Thoughts of today

Swift and Swirled

Swirled and Swift

They jump from start to finish

I should be thinking

Of laughter, of heartache

Of philosophy

Of music to play

I should be reminiscing of successes

Or lamenting regresses

A distant echo of a train's whistle

Breaks my swift and swirled thoughts

What of the day

Got to go

Someone's calling

I should be writing

Me thinks

There's always tomorrow

If not for today

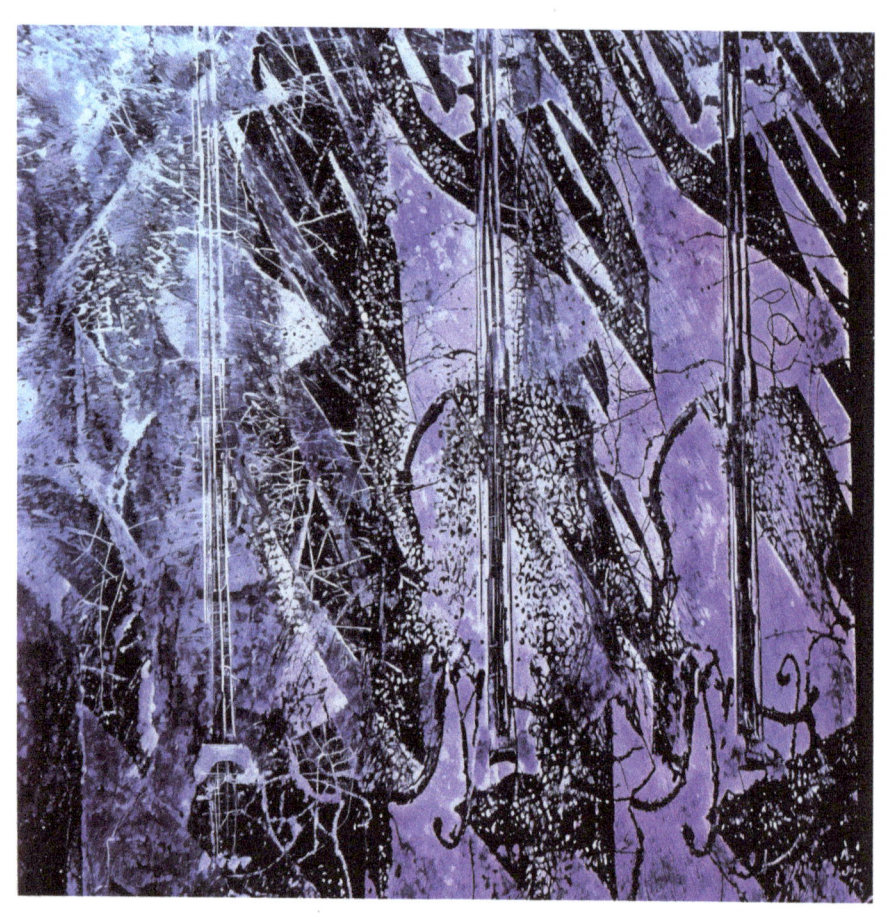

Purple Violins

Computer Graphic design

Hand drawn with the mouse

I call it "Mouse Art."

I SHOULD BE SINGING

I should be singing

I should be singing of songs of peace

Songs of courage

And songs of love

A song about the oceans

May they never run dry

A song from the heart that tells no lies

Is there a memory that I can recall

A scripture that gives me hope

I can hear the melody of the wind

Whistling in the trees

Or the bumble bee kisses

As he lights a dandelion, a rose

Clover as It tickles his toes

He can sleep now

He can dream

Of someone singing

A melody, his song

His longing for someone

A special someone

Who will sing him his song

CELEBRATION BIG SUR

ESALEN INSTITUTE MONTEREY, CALIFORNIA

In the summer of 1969, the Esalen Institute in Monterey, California, became the backdrop for one of the most significant moments of my career: *Celebration Big Sur*. The event itself was more than a performance—it was a fusion of art, music, and spirit, a place where artists gathered to express the countercultural energy of the times. Little did I know it would also be my gateway into a world of musical legends. I had just turned nineteen when fate seemed to intervene. John Allen Astin—yes, the same John Astin who played Gomez on *The Addams Family*, the classic black comedy—heard me singing along the San Antonio RiverWalk. His presence was unexpected, and in hindsight, it feels almost surreal, like the universe was opening a door for me. John Astin didn't just listen to me—he acted. He informed Milan Melvin, who at the time was married to Mimi Farina, Joan Baez's sister. Before I knew it, both Milan and Mimi had come to hear me sing. I still remember the butterflies in my stomach, knowing they were watching. As I later learned, they were looking for a young singer to become Joan Baez's protégé, and somehow, that young singer turned out to be me. "Not long after, I received an invitation that would change everything—I was asked to perform at the legendary Monterey Pop Festival, specifically *Celebration Big Sur*. This event wasn't just another festival; it was a cultural phenomenon. Later, it would even be immortalized on film, a movie that still bears the name *Celebration Big Sur*. Little did I know at the time that this performance would become a defining moment in my life and career.

For my set, I chose two songs close to my heart—'La Paloma' and 'La Malagueña Salerosa,' traditional Mexican ballads that carried the weight of my heritage. I sang them with every fiber of my being, but nothing could have prepared me for what came next. As I finished the last note, a wave of applause erupted, and I saw a crowd of five thousand people rise to their feet, offering me a standing ovation. The shock was written all over my face. Even now, when I watch the footage, I can still see the surprise, the disbelief, the joy. They truly connected with these songs, with me, and I was deeply moved.

I can still vividly recall meeting Joan Baez and Joni Mitchell. At that moment, it felt like I was living in a dream. These weren't just singers—they were two of my greatest musical influences, women whose voices had shaped the very fabric of my own artistry. To say I was star-struck would be an understatement. How often do we get to meet our heroes? And yet, there I was, standing in the presence of two legends. It was humbling, it was exhilarating, and utterly surreal. The lineup of talent that day was nothing short of iconic. Joan Baez, Joni Mitchell, John Sebastian, Dorothy Morison, Sal Valentino, and then, of course, the legends of Crosby, Stills, Nash, and Young. It was a gathering of some of the greatest voices of a generation, artists whose music defined an era. To be in their company felt like an honor beyond words.

I found myself sitting next to John Sebastian, right there on stage. The ground at our feet was littered with cigarette butts—something I hadn't paid much attention to at first. But curiosity got the better of me, and I turned to him and asked, 'What kind of cigarette butts are these?' I had never seen marijuana joints before, so I had no idea. His reaction was priceless. He just stared at me for a second, then gave me this look as if to say, 'Are you serious?' He didn't say a word—just shook his head and ignored me. At the time, I didn't understand his reaction, but looking back, I can't help but laugh at how out of place my question must have seemed in that setting. Couldn't figure out why at the time. It's funny how some fun memories stick in your mind and how rude he was. Other than that, it was an incredible experience. Joni Mitchell and Joan Baez were gracious and wonderful.

Today, the magic of that moment lives on. *Celebration Big Sur* was eventually made into a movie, and now it's available for anyone to watch on YouTube or Google. I sometimes find myself revisiting it, letting the memories wash over me—the music, the people, the energy of that place and time. It's incredible to know that something I was a part of continues to inspire others, even decades later.

Celebration "Big Sur"

Steven Stills, Myself, John Sebastian, and Mimi Farina

On our way to the stage

Los Angeles Free Press

September 19, 1969

Rolling Stone

Oct. 18, 1969

27

Joan Baez & Myself

Celebration Big Sur

Photo

Joni Mitchell & Myself

Celebration Big Sur

Photo

The Poppies

Acrylic Alcohol Ink

30

LA LA LAND
The City of Lost Angels

In 1970, I packed up my life in San Antonio and set out for Los Angeles—the so-called 'City of Lost Angels.' Little did I know the dream I was chasing would come with a rude awakening. The glittering lights and promises of fame masked a gritty underworld dominated by music and entertainment agencies, and I was about to get a harsh introduction. I still remember walking into that room for the first time. There he was—a greasy, overweight man with a pasty face, the kind of smug SOB I hadn't even imagined encountering. He looked me up and down like I was nothing, just another hopeful kid trying to make it in a world that chews people up and spits them out. I guess I didn't have enough confidence to seek out more reputable agencies. When I showed him my high school picture. he laughed and replied, "Don't you have any sexy pictures of yourself?" He made it clear as he showed me a picture of a blond whose boobs were popping out and me. "How was I ever going to get a gig with that innocent picture? I was just a young girl with stars in her eyes, untouched by the gritty realities of this world. It didn't take long to realize that, according to his standards, my dreams didn't stand a chance. No club would book me—not unless I conformed to their twisted expectations. Reality does bite, and when it bites, it sinks its teeth in deep.

But, the one thing that I was always blessed with was associating myself with great musicians. Billy Childs was a friend of mine. Wherever I went, there was always a helping hand and good friend. I was able to create, paint, sketch, write a poem or a song; these intermediate moments kept me sane.

After performing at Celebration Big Sur for the second time, I found myself traveling from LA to San Francisco, where I stayed with Milan Melvin and Mimi Farina. Their home was a refuge, a place filled with music, art, and a sense of community that fed my soul during those tumultuous years. Heard about the "The Great American Medicine Ball Caravan" 1970, a Warner Bros. Production tour of 150 hippies traveling from San Francisco throughout America, Boulder, Colorado, Antioch, Ohio, Washington DC at the Sunset Monument, and the Washington Monument. It's final destination is the Isle of Wight Festival, England. I was lucky enough to be one of the warm-up acts. Just me and my guitar, standing on stage before crowds who were there to see legends like The Youngbloods, Jefferson Airplane, and even Alice Cooper, who headlined in Washington, DC. It was surreal—little old me, playing before these giants of rock. But in those moments, I felt like I belonged. After DC, we moved on to New York and, eventually, England. It was more than just a tour—it became a part of history. The Great American Cannonball Express—as the trip was later called—has since been immortalized in literature. The book America, We've Come for Your Daughters captured the essence of that wild journey, a snapshot of a generation that was pushing boundaries and searching for something more. What a party.

THE GREAT AMERICAN
CANNON BALL EXPRESS

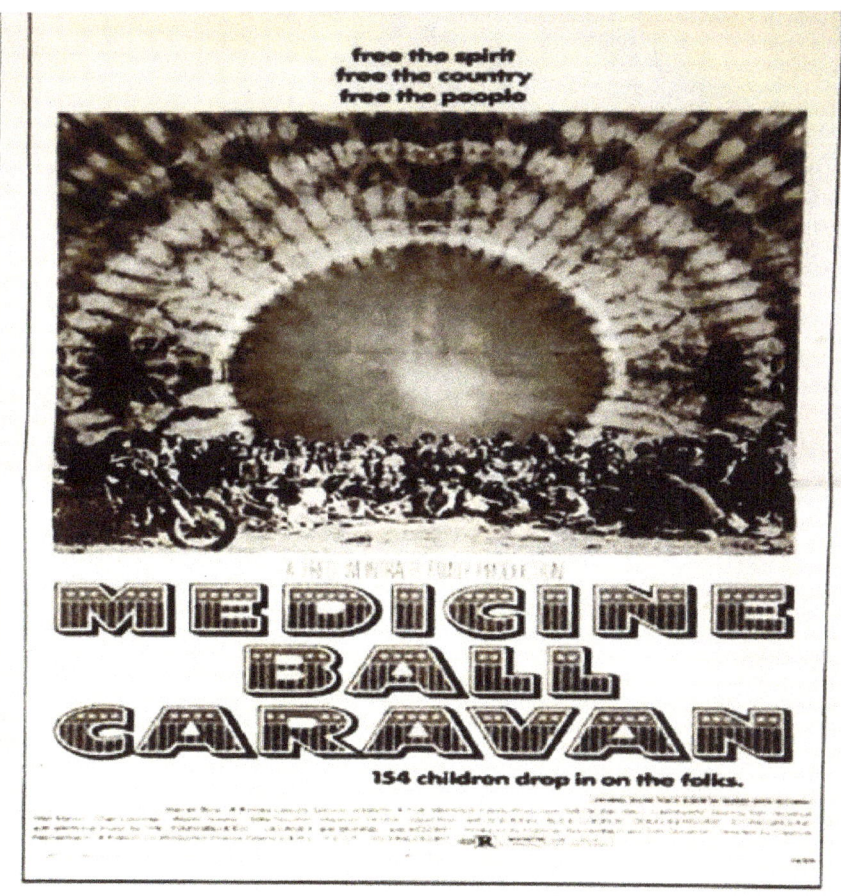

1971, After Big Sur, I accidentally fell into an opportunity to travel with a "Warner Brothers, Francois Reichenbach, a French director with (according to the Warner Brothers publicity sheet) a "crack 15-man film crew" and two studio accountants." from the New York Times August 26, 2015.

The New York Times
Wednesday, August 26, 2015

Movies

• Movies   All NYT   Search

WORLD   U.S.   N.Y./REGION   BUSINESS   TECHNOLOGY   SCIENCE   HEALTH   SPORTS   OPINION   ARTS   STYLE   TRAVEL   **JOBS**   **REAL ESTATE**   **AUTOS**

Search Movies or Showtimes by ZIP Code

More in Movies »
In Theaters   Coming Soon   Critics' Picks   On DVD   Tickets & Showtimes   Trailers   ArtsBeat

Tickets & Showtimes

Enter your ZIP code or city to view tickets and showtimes in your area.

Overview

Tickets & Showtimes

New York Times Review

Cast, Credits & Awards

MOVIE REVIEW

Medicine Ball Caravan (1971)
'Medicine Ball Caravan' Bows:Free-Wheeling Bus Is Followed Across U.S.

By ROGER GREENSPUN
Published: August 26, 1971

TWITTER
LINKEDIN
E-MAIL
PRINT
SHARE

City, State or ZIP   Submit

More Theaters Near You »

mistress america now playing

"Medicine Ball Caravan," which opened yesterday at the Plaza, is the filmed account of a free-spirited bus trip made last summer by 150-odd beautiful people, counter-culturists, musicians, Hog Farmers, hangers-on and hip entrepreneurs. Also along, not exactly for the ride, were assorted journalists, François Reichenbach, a French director, with (according to the Warner Brothers publicity sheet) a "crack 15-man film crew," and two studio accountants. For this last information I am indebted not to Warner Brothers but to Ron Rosenbaum, a Village Voice reporter, whose eyewitness articles on the caravan make an essential accompaniment to the movie.

Led, more or less, by an immense, bearded, deep-voiced, aging disk jockey named Tom Donahue, the caravan set out from San Francisco in silver-painted buses carrying tie-dyed tepees, headed for points east (and eventually, the Isle of Wight) with the intention of giving concerts, confronting middle America, and incidentally making a movie. The movie begins in San Francisco, as, on the sound track, a choir of heavenly voices sings over the head of Tom Donahue in his broadcasting studio. But it ends, a little abruptly, at Antioch College in Ohio, where there was a confrontation, but not the one that had been expected.

The ostensible reason for the caravan was, of course, to present concerts. What you see of the concerts seems to have little enough to do with the caravan. For the most part they feature imported big-name talent, B. B. King, Doug Kershaw, etc., and they are treated by Reichenbach as isolated, self-contained events. On the other hand, there are the caravan's "events": bathing in a giant bowl of Jello prepared by Wavey Gravey and the Hog Farm, pacifying the violent STP Family in Boulder, answering the activists at Antioch.

The caravan's real problems came not from middle America, which, according to the evidence on the screen, seemed downright chummy, but from the youthful political left, who is, despite a certain amount of camouflage, saw Warner Brothers and smelled a rat. Along the way an activist named David Peel attached himself to the caravan with the purpose of exposing it, and at Antioch there occurred a series of misadventures leading to guerrilla theater, a nontheatrical knife attack on Peel and much violent argument over the not so profitable question of who was bought and who had sold, between the movie company and the counter-culture, who was ripping off whom.

In a way, but then I would normally side against the movie company. The staged confrontation is perhaps on the whole an interesting bore. But the concluding confrontations

I was a part of 156 Hippies, free-spirited and the counterculture of America at that time. There were musicians, "Wavy Gravy and the Hog Farmers," journalists and me, traveling From San Francisco, Boulder, Colorado, Phoenix, Arizona, Antioch, Ohio, Washington DC, Washington, and finally, the Isle of Wight Festival. I was one of the warm-up acts to BB King, Doug Kershaw, Alice Cooper, etc., I didn't even know that I was a "Hippie." It was an inspirational time. A time of discovery, awareness, a spiritual and meta-physical awakening. And although I didn't smoke pot, I did experiment with hallucinogenic magic mushrooms mystical Psilocybin, where sight, smell, taste, and even touch were altered. Where you hear colors, see music, and taste the rainbow. I also tried LSD, which was a very scary journey, and never again... It was a Carlos Castaneda dream world, an altered state of mind. Most of the time, I was stoned.

It was the early 70s, this was a time when many Americans were looking for another reality, because the reality of that time was not working for them. The endless Vietnam War, racial strife, segregation, and the inequality of the rich versus the middle class and the poor. We defined a decade with three days of free music, tie-dyed tee pees, random nudity, and a lot of pot, reefer, marijuana. It was one big party.

We traveled in U-Hauls, Rider trucks, Winnebago(s), and painted buses. I was in the "Big Bertha Bus." One of the experiences I remember was in Antioch, where there was a political and violent argument; David Peel, an English actor, was attacked by the political left. In the meantime, "Big Bertha" had almost fallen into a crevasse. "Mouse," the driver was trying desperately to get the bus out. We were on the bus, looking out the window, laughing, and wondering what was going on. Why we didn't have the sense to get out, I'll never know. But he did manage to get "Big Bertha" out of danger.

Warner had provided us with a round-trip ticket home from England. I missed the Isle Wight Festival due to the fact that my passport was delayed one day. The last concert of this extraordinary trip was a final concert in Hyde Park, London, England.

War and Eric Burdon were on stage. I was underneath the stage with a rather handsome guy who turned me on to hashish and only wanted to kiss me. I was drawn, like a moth to a flame, to the music which was happening on stage. It was "War," and Eric Burdon singing "Spill the Wine," I was able to go on stage since I was one of the entertainers. I found myself between the bass player and the conga player, who kept smiling at me. I could see lightning coming from his congas to the bass player's amp.

I also sang in the subways of London. Good money; the passersby would give me five pounds at a time, and in American currency, that would be twice as much at that time. I would usually walk out with at least a hundred dollars or $50.00 in pounds. But the Bobbies, London's subway police, came and got me and explained that the skinheads would come and get my money, my instrument, beat me, and leave me for dead. That was the end of the London subways and the Caravan. Soon after, I just wanted to go home. Too many weirdos.

others, but that's about it, not counting the rather undistinguished Stoneground, the traveling "house and" that would later be responsible for providing three-fourths of the lineup for Pablo Cruise. If the udio had snagged their first choice, a Warner-Reprise act called the Grateful Dead, "MBC" would likely ot be so obscure.

was generally believed that the studio execs, by sending this freak circus out into the land of the Silent lajority, were hoping for some sort of climatic cinematic confrontation. But most of the straights that eichenbach shows are cordial if not supportive while any conflicts in the film emanate from within the iravan's own demographic. There's a tense run-in with the Manson-lite STP Family at the Boulder, olorado show and chaotic confrontations on the campus of Ohio's Antioch College before a proposed oncert nearby. There had been grumblings all summer from the New Left that Medicine Ball was a Warn rothers scam, a ploy to usurp the counterculture by getting naïve hedonists to play act a plastic version (

espite the fact that caravaners were only being paid expenses and counted among their number such bo des as Wavy Gravy, suspicions about this "sell out" were exploited by provocateurs-without-portfolio avid Peel and Tom Forcade, the latter of whom had been nipping at the heels of Tom Donahue weeks fore they reached Antioch. Humorless young campus radicals were whipped into hysteria over the otion that corporate suits (AKA "capitalist pigs") would dare make a movie that may appeal to some in eir age group. In the fracas that followed, these summer-program students ("kept in school by their arents to keep them away from home," says one caravan wag) try to shut down the show, forcing the aveling troupe to stand up for themselves, and defend their efforts to work within the system to spread e peace-and-love message. Suddenly, "Medicine Ball Caravan" turns contentious and interesting, but b en it's almost over.

https://rickouelletteredandrock.files.wordpress.com/2015/03/the_hog_farm_bus.jpg)

our ride is here

Emily Rose

Beautiful Child

oil

BEAUTIFUL CHILD

Beautiful Child, where will you go?

Will there still be a beautiful sky

And beautiful butterflies

Do you know how to fly?

Beautiful Child, what will you see?

Rainbows and Raindrops

And a sunrise that beams

Will you still be able to taste

Sweet nectar from the honey bees?

Beautiful Child, what will you hear?

The rustling of leaves

The wind in the trees

Will there be stars in the sky?

Stars in your eyes?

Dreams of oceans, rivers, and sunlit streams?

Will your guardians have a watchful eye?

Will there be loved ones to help you on your way?

And to help you earnestly

To achieve your dreams?

Beautiful Child, what will you do?

The future, you know

It is up to you.

Emily Rose

In Her Goth Period

oil

EMILY ROSE

Emily Rose is the cherished daughter of my best friend, Karen. From the moment she was born, Emily's life seemed destined for challenges, beginning with an event that could have taken everything from her. When she was just a baby, she came perilously close to death. She was in a horrific car crash, an accident in which her baby carriage was thrown from the car and landed by a rural farm fence. Emily was finally found after several hours by one of the detectives who heard a baby crying. Even at an early age, Emily possessed an unshakable will to survive, a fierce determination for life that has only grown stronger with time. That same inner drive shines through her in everything she does. You can see it in her radiant aura, in the way she pours her soul into the violin when she plays, and in the way she lives and loves with a fullness that touches everyone around her, especially those closest to her heart. Emily particularly loves animals, especially dogs. She is an inspiration to me and to all who dearly love her. If I were to sum up Emily in just a few words, it would be this: 'Grace in Motion.' She moves through life with a quiet elegance, a strength that never wavers, and a heart full of compassion. In everything she does—whether it's playing her violin, loving her family, or simply being herself—there is grace.

THE THREE EMILY (S)

Emily Rose 1

"Contemplation"

Acrylic Alcohol Ink

and acrylic paint

Emily ll

"Emily in the Garden"

Acrylic Alcohol Ink

and acrylic paint

Emily lll

"Relaxed"

Acrylic Alcohol Ink

and acrylic paint

45

THE POWER OF HANDS

There is an undeniable power in the human touch, a power that can heal wounds we cannot see, that can inspire the building of monuments, and that can evoke pure joy and wonder in the heart of a child. From a simple caress to a hand wiping away tears, the power of touch is transformative. It speaks volumes where words fail, and it connects us in ways nothing else can. How incredibly powerful is the human touch, capable of softening hearts and bridging gaps between souls. Hands have the ability to reach out and make an impact, often in ways we don't even realize. A single touch can spark a ripple of change, a transfer of energy that softens even the hardest of hearts. It's an exchange of synergy, an electric current that has the power to turn an angry mobster into a gentle, loveable teddy bear. The human touch can break down barriers, transform anger into affection, and create an invisible bond of trust and care.

It's said that babies, and even animals, who are deprived of touch—left isolated from the warmth of human connection—can grow up to face challenges such as autism or emotional detachment. There's something profound in the way touch nurtures development, how it generates an unseen electricity that fosters growth, healing, and security. This simple act of human connection, a touch, holds within it the power to soothe fears, spark life, and cultivate a foundation of trust. We are electric.

About two years ago, I had an ablation to my heart. It was racing and created pain as well as lethargy. My doctor explained that the electrical currents from the upper top of my heart were not going to the lower part of my heart. WOW, I thought, I am an electric being. We are all electric beings. Life can be so amazing.

Hands that play guitar, piano, or any instrument. Hands that can paint and build a house, an Empire, the San Francisco State Bridge.

There's a power that exists between two beings, a power so potent that it has the ability to create life itself. In the sacred union of two souls, the energy exchanged can bring forth the miracle of a child. But with that same power to create love, there lies the opposite—the power to destroy. It's a delicate balance, a choice we all face in every action we take. My hope is that we choose love so that we recognize the immense potential within us to build up rather than tear down.

There is a place called heaven, and sometimes, if we're lucky, it reaches down and touches Earth in the simplest of ways — a blessing, a kind smile, or even the gentle press of a kiss. In those moments, we catch glimpses of something greater, something pure and divine. These fleeting touches of heaven remind us that beauty, love, and grace can be found in the most ordinary of things if only we stop to notice them.

Karen

Sitting in a Field of Poppies

oil

SISTER*SOUL

Karen Barrs Bullard, mother of Emily Rose and my dearest friend for over 30 years, has always been there for me, especially through times of hardship. We laughed so hard till it hurt, cried, and painted. "Sister*Soul" is what she called us. We created six large paintings and 6-8 pillow cases. At the time, Karen was going through one of the most challenging periods of her life—a devastating divorce. She was working as an airline stewardess with Continental Airlines, juggling the demands of her job while trying to hold herself together in the midst of heartbreak. Through it all, she showed a strength and grace that I still admire to this day. When she was working, her husband was an alcoholic but a very charming and handsome alcoholic, one night he went to his favorite bar in New Braunfels, where he took Emily. She must have been one or two. On the way home, driving on the wrong side of a farm road, he had a terrible accident. He was sent to prison with a scared face. Emily was thrown from the car. She was in her baby carrier until the detectives heard a baby crying. Her baby carriage was thrown from the car where it hit a fence. She nearly died that day. But lived. Her determination in life was amazing. Karen was devastated.

As I was getting ready for major surgery, Complete Bi-lateral Hip Surgery. Karen and I created several large paintings together. "Sister*Soul" It was an initial interest in creativity, pop art, and abstract expressionist "Dream Pillows and Dream Pillow Cases," as well as several large paintings. A very personal expression of our dreams. Karen referred to them "as 'dysfunctional, beautiful to look at, but impractical to use."

PAINTED PILLOW CASES

front

back

THE SISTER SOUL COLLECTION

SISTER * SOUL

ream   Pillows*
ream PIllow Cases &
r   e   a   m   s   *
Karen   Barrs   and   Caro
Cisneros   co-founded   Sister*Soul.
With an initial interest in creativity,
pop art, and abstract expressionism,
they have created a very personal
expressionofDreamPillows,Dream
Pillow cases & Dreams. Ms. Barrs
refers   to   these   pillow   cases
" d y s f u n c t i o n a
"Beautifultolookat,butimpractical
to use." We sincerely hope this art
will give everyone inspiration and
c   r   e   a   t   i   v   e

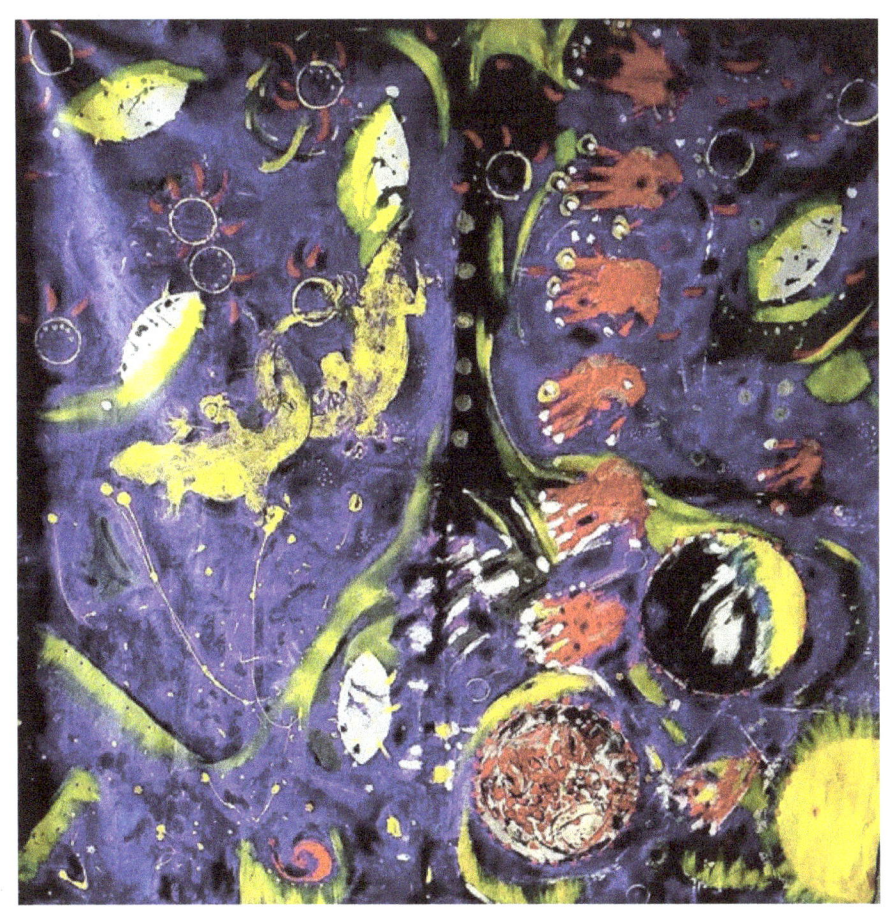

Inner Sporangium Opus 42

From the Sister Soul Collection

Acrylic

4"X4

South Texas Night on the Fourth of July

From the Sister Soul Collection

Acrylic

4"X4

"I Woke Up This Morning With My Picasso Face"

From the Sister Soul Collection

Acrylic

4"X4"

KERRVILLE FOLK FESTIVAL
OUTDOOR THEATER

QUIET VALLEY RANCH KERRVILLE, TX

In 1975, I was invited to sing at the Kerrville Folk Festival, May 22 -25, Outdoor Theater in Quiet Valley Ranch Kerrville, Texas. I performed two more Festivals at Kerrville the following years. Not sure of the dates.

Beer Mugs

Rice Paper Painting

Iridescent Ink & Oil Pastels

1978, Awarded for my composition *"Recruerdame"* ("Remember Me") El Festival OTI-USA, Miami, Florida. KWEX -DT channel 42, a television station in San Antonio. Unfortunately, the person who invited me did not understand what a music arrangement was, so before we got to the OTI FestivalMiami, I had asked her, "Who will do the arrangement for my composition?" She thought I was talking about who will take us to the airport, who will drive us to the festival, where we will stay, etc. So, when it was my turn to perform, I didn't have a music arrangement for the orchestra. Everyone else did. I remember "Jose Jose" asked me what happened. When I told him, he just shook his head and replied, "Que lastima," which meant "What a Pity" in English. I wrote out a chart for the rhythm section, the piano player, bass player, and drummer who accompanied me as I played my guitar. It actually was very special. "What the heck happened?' Another life lesson.

In 2005, published in the International Library of Poetry, *Twilight Musings*, Howard Ely, Editor, Poetry.com

From 2010 - 2020 I was a resident artist at the Bihl Haus Art featured in their yearly catalogs.

Wolf & Cat

oil Pastels

CHARLIE THE TREE

I've often imagined trees

the lungs of the world,

typing away in their cubicles

One day, one of the trees

I'll call him Charlie

One day, Charlie decided that he

was tired of being a telemarketer

and decided to leave, just walk out

As he ventured out

Into the vast world of humanity

He traveled along the path

of a stream, and as it got bigger

and became a river

The sun lit its running waters with diamonds

He liked it so much

That he decided to plant himself right there.

Charlie thought to himself

This is so beautiful here

I'll always have enough water

to sustain myself and become strong

I'll lift my branches upward

To the sky, always giving praise and thanks to the Universe

I'll even make a home for the birds, the small animals,

and the little critters

And for the people, I'll give them oxygen

he so often heard and saw to it

That there would be fruit for all to eat

If someone cuts off one of the branches

I'll grow two

this was the tale of Charlie the Tree,

Who finally found his place in the universe.

"EXPO SAN ANTONIO EN MEXICO"

February 20th, 1982

EXPO SAN ANTONIO EN MEXICO CITY

Steve Rose, Bob Shoaf, James Paul Kalson Jr, myself, Ronnie Wilkins, Earnest Taylor, Cecil Carter

Truly remarkable musicians and friends. I was so blessed to be a part of this group. There is nothing better than to travel with those musicians you respect and love you and your music. How blessed my life has been.

Golden Violins

Acrylic Alcohol Ink

At a Moment's Notice

The wind shifts,

So does the moving sand

With this intensity

You could crack a diamond in your hand

You could rid the world of crime

Maybe even stop time

An ever-faint echo of a helping hand

Cries out, "You are my hero,

In a world filled with so much sorrow, so much pain."

"All are heavy-hearted in this sinking sand."

Chief Smiling Lizard sings his song of woe

Silently, he sways into the blue crimson night

And so we make love at a moment's notice

And with a silent glance

You free my spirit

And once again

I learn to dance.

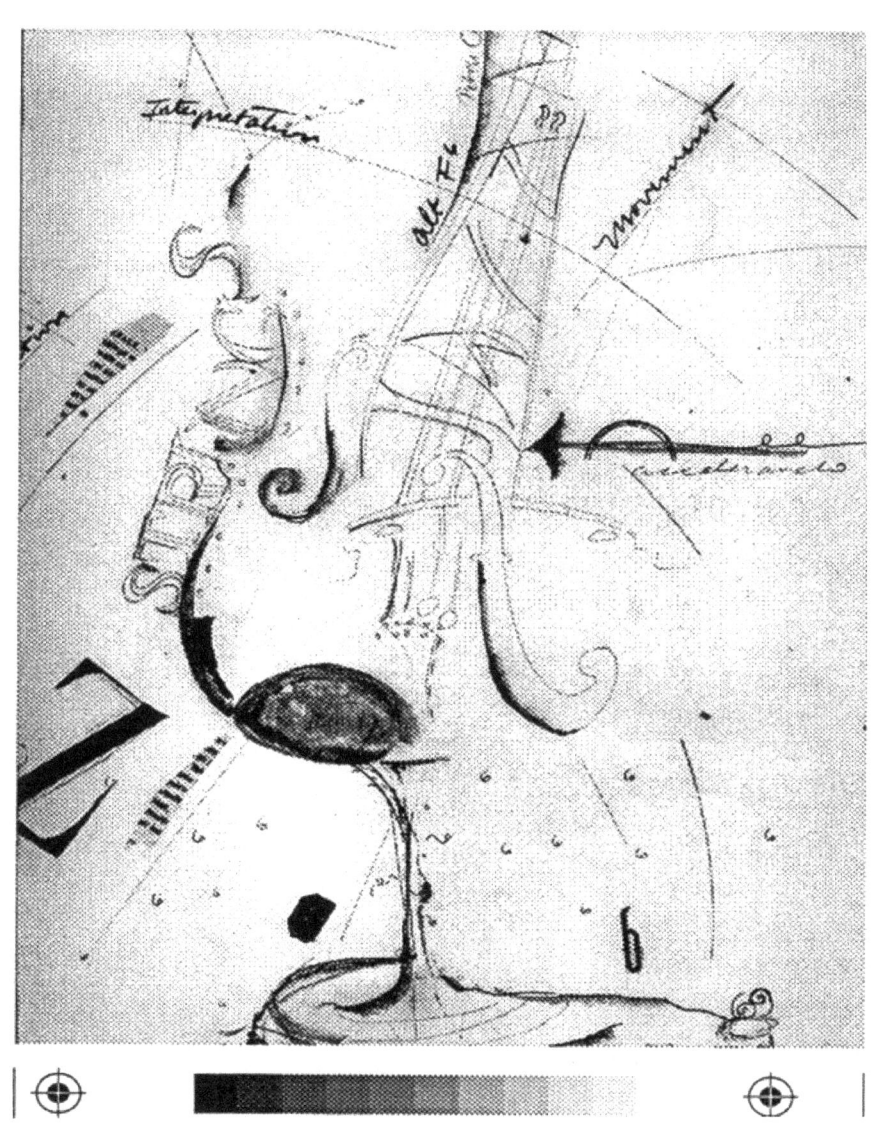

Goofy Image Jazz & Strings

Graphite

QUESTIONS ASKED

Am I shallow? Am I weak

Am I strong, maybe even deep?

Does it matter when I speak?

Question asked when I sleep.

Do you see me dreaming?

Dogs barking, walls creaking.

Morning comes; someone's speaking.

And still more questions asked.

Hurray For another day!

Abstractions of Color

Oil on Rice Paper Collage

LA LOBOTOMY

My mind is drained

I'm feeling no pain

To me, it feel like a hurricane

I been hit by a Freight train

I've been hypnotized

Sanitized

Homogenized

Past - your eyes

Too much pollution

Evokes evolution

I'm in a Fred Astaire state

Can You Relate

Let's all integrate

Cause we're on our way to London

Johannesburg and France

Let's all get up and do a little dance

La Lobotomy

Hey, is this a party

Or is this a wake?

Cause a man without Education.

Is like a tree without leaves

In Jamaica, there's a tree

That bleeds every Easter

La Lobotomy, Hey!

"Is this a party, or is this a Wake?"

A Puffin Bird, A Duck & Fish all Around

THE VOID MOON & THE NEGATIVE FOOL

The negative pool is filled with the negative fools

Trying to find a negative place

Living in the void of a negative life

Living in the void of the negative space

Linear, dissonant, backup water, a sludge void of humanity.

Does one know could it be the status quo

Whatever it is,

One came to do

Even when they choose to do

Or not to do

We do

All are actors meshed in the cosmic world

Sinking to the bottom of the murky swirl

Gnashing little fumes

Filled with a negative cesspool

Woes that eclipses the sun and moon

A bloom that never grows

A rose that never blooms

Blissful moments of amalgamated static sounds

Well, where should we send these clowns

Perhaps one day, we'll see this Negative Fool

And send them back

To the void moon & the negative pool

Back Home Again, San Antonio

University of Texas in San Antonio

Back Home

There are other realities

Though I've been told

I am a musician and an artist

My life just turned out that way

Started out one way and ended up another

Just a figment of imagination

Guess I'll just doodle my way

Back Home.

DR. CHARLES FIELD
Continued my career as a visual artist

My journey as a visual artist truly began with formal studies in Fine Art under the guidance of Dr. Charles Field at the University of Texas, San Antonio. From 1991 to 1994, I deepened my exploration of the visual arts, continuing my education at Southwest Texas State University (now Texas State University), where I studied advanced printmaking under the brilliant Dr. Eric Neilson. Each step in my artistic development felt like peeling back a new layer, revealing more about myself, my culture, and the world around me. I found endless inspiration in the works of the great abstract expressionists—Miro, Kandinsky, Klee, and Rothko. Their ability to evoke emotion and movement through color and form ignited something in me. But my artistic influences didn't stop there. I also drew from the genius of Norman Rockwell, J.M.W. Turner, and the timeless masterpieces of Picasso, Rembrandt, Cezanne, Michelangelo, and countless others. Each artist brought something unique, a different way of seeing the world, and in their work, I found pieces of myself. For me, art is more than just a visual representation—it's a window into my soul, an expression of dreams and the intangible. Through my work, I try to capture the fluidity of emotion, the shifting perspectives, and the ever-changing moods that define our human experience. My pieces are often abstractions, allowing viewers to perceive their own realities through the shapes, colors, and forms I create. It's a dialogue between the art, myself, and the observer—each bringing something unique to the interpretation. As a Mexican/American Women, I've incorporated both my heritage along with my musical experiences, an unique combination I call my "Mexican Soul," My love of America and my Mexican Heritage and all that it stands for inspires and moves me to create both my art and my music. This is not just what I try to do. It is who I am; It is a part of my DNA.

And although I am legally disabled and live with chronic pain for over twenty years, I continues to pursue as much as I can with both the arts & music. I am passionate about the arts.

South West Texas

now, Texas State University

San Marcos, Texas

Dr. Eric Neilson

Advanced Printmaking

One of my favorite teacher at Southwest Texas State University, which later was called the University of Texas, San Marcos, was Dr. Eric Neilson, advanced printmaking. Perhaps my love for printmaking stems from the endless possibilities it offers. Whether I was working on an etching, a linoleum block relief, or a serigraph, each piece felt like a new adventure, an exploration of variations on a theme. There's something comforting in the repetition, the refinement, in the way a single idea can evolve into countless forms. Printmaking allowed me to express myself in ways that felt both structured and free, a combination that brought me peace during times of turmoil. During that period, I was also pursuing my love of jazz singing, studying under Dr. James Polk— who had worked closely with the legendary Ray Charles. However, my journey took a painful detour when I was involved in a car accident that left me with a broken collarbone and an injured back. The physical pain was overwhelming, but it was in the act of creation that I found solace. Art, especially printmaking, became a form of therapy, a way to channel the pain into something beautiful. Getting involved and lost in color, lines, and balance was therapeutic.

Tres Hermanas

Linoleum Relief printed on Dark Blue Paper

Real flowers collage painted pink

Painted Flowers

Tres Hermanas

Linoleum Block Print Relief

Oil Pastel

Tres Hermanas

Faith Hope & Charity

Vinyl Print Relief

Tres Hermanas

Vinyl Print Relief

Limited Edition

Jazz Musicians & Jazz Angels

Jean-phillip Rominger, Jay Fort, Armin Marmolejo

& Jerry Madrigal

Acrylic

4'X4'

SOUTH TEXAS GIRL

She's just a South Texas Girl
Livin' the hard life easy
She's got the summer wind in her hair
And the South Texas Sun on her face
She's just a lonesome, mournful dove
Waiting for her true love
But there's no place she'd rather be
Then kickin' it with you and with me
She's been to Nueva York
Amsterdam and Paree'
She's drivin' her GMC Jimmy
With her love by her side
There playing Count Basie, Dylan, Whalin'
And Ray Charles, too
And on the radio, Ellington Swings
And in the country, the mockingbird sings
With the Jasmine' in her hair
And the Blue Bonnets everywhere
And though the Summer nights are hot
She'll be cool at her favorite jazz spot
She is just a lonesome, mournful dove
Waiting for her true love
But there's no place she'd rather be
Then kickin' it with you and with me.

MY TIME ON THE SAN ANTONIO RIVERWALK

I began singing professionally at just sixteen, a time when most teenagers were still figuring out who they were while I was already discovering my voice. Right after my time with the Glee Club at Central Catholic High School, I'd head down to the San Antonio Riverwalk, back when it was still a hidden gem, far from the bustling tourist attraction it is today. Beneath the bridges, where the water echoed softly against the stone, I'd open my guitar case and sing, letting the music carry through the quiet evenings. There was something magical about that place—the way the setting sun reflected off the water, the stillness of the night. I was surprised, even touched, when people passing by would pause to listen, then toss money into my guitar case as though they could sense the passion I poured into each note. The ambeince was pretty awesome. I was surprised that passersby would throw money into my guitar case. My first official gig was at the Hilton Palacio Del Rio, a moment that felt like I was stepping into a whole new world. I performed there for over a year, and during that time, I was also fortunate enough to sing at the HemisFair '69 World's Fair at the charming La Maison Blanche, a French restaurant nestled in the heart of San Antonio. I still remember the food—the rich flavors of French cuisine that I had never tasted before. It was a feast for both my voice and my palate, an experience that felt as grand and international as the event itself. As time passed, I found myself getting more gigs around the River Walk, each one adding a new layer to my growing career. One of my favorite spots was the River Roost, a cozy venue that became a second home for my music. It was there that I met Richard Brown, a man whose quiet strength and musical talent left a lasting impression on me. He would show up with his bass, harmonica, or sometimes a dulcimer, and we'd create spontaneous harmonies that felt effortless as if our souls were communicating through the music. Those moments weren't just performances; they were collaborations that nurtured something special in both of us. I didn't even know he was in the military and an entomologist at Fort Sam Houston.

Richard and I became very close as an entomologist. We became very close and, through the years, have kept in touch. One of my most cherished memories with Richard was the time I traveled to Washington, DC, where he was working in the Smithsonian's entomology department. By day, he'd be absorbed in his work, and I'd lose myself wandering through the various Smithsonian museums, taking in all the art and history they had to offer. My favorite was the Post-Impressionist building, where I stood in awe before masterpieces that I had only ever seen in books. But the real magic happened after hours. Richard would show me the city as it came alive at night, its monuments glowing in the darkness, each one telling a story of its own. Those quiet moments, exploring the heart of the nation's capital with him, felt like something out of a dream. One day, we decided to travel up to New York on black mollys. Oh boy, never do that again. Honestly, at the time, it was fun. I was still young then. I can't remember when I had a better time. We spent our days wandering the streets of New York, eating at some of the best delis and restaurants the city had to offer. Each meal felt like a discovery, a new taste of a city that was as alive as we were. But my favorite memory by far was the time I played and sang in Greenwich Village, a place that had seen countless artists before me. Standing there with my guitar, performing in such a legendary spot, I felt connected to something much bigger than myself—a history of musicians and storytellers who had come before me, filling the streets with their songs. We had picked up a friend of his, and later, on the way to Long Island, where his friend lived, I took my turn to drive. And, of course, I got lost and wound up in a small rural town where we ran out of gas. It was around five in the morning, the kind of early hour where the world felt quiet and still. We stumbled upon a small diner, the only place open, and decided to grab breakfast. I don't remember exactly what Richard said—it was something simple, maybe even absurd—but it sent me into a fit of laughter. The kind of laughter that's uncontrollable, where tears stream down your face and your sides ache. Soon, we were all laughing, causing such a scene that the manager kindly asked us to leave. It was one of those moments where the laughter was louder than the situation, where joy took over, and nothing else mattered. We were still waiting for the gas station across the street to open. Richard messed with the sign, and luckily, we left before anyone could read it. I was a wild child then, but with my friend, who was very conservative, we got away with a little mischief. Looking back, it was too much fun, the kind of fun that only comes with the freedom of youth and the company of a true friend. Even now, after all these years, Richard and I have remained lifelong friends. The memories we share, the laughter, the misadventures—they've woven a bond that time hasn't touched.

Richard Brown & Myself

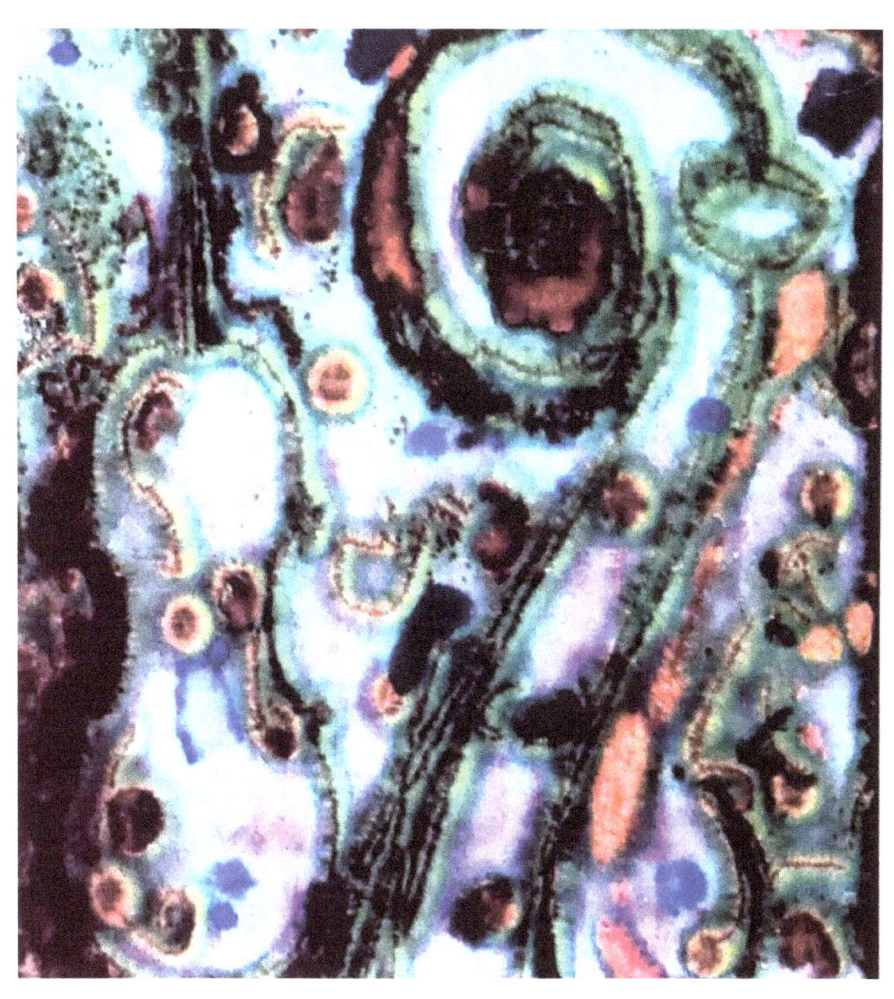

Violins

Graphic Design

One of my most memorable gigs was at a BBQ restaurant and bar called 1836, a place where I found myself constantly pushing my limits. The restaurant sat just above the River Walk, and I loved the challenge of seeing how many people I could lure in from below. With speakers set up outside, my voice would drift down to the passersby, drawing them in like a siren's call. It wasn't just about performing—it was about connecting with people, pulling them in with nothing but the power of music. Since the club was upstairs, with the speakers outside on the patio, my voice was aired outside for passerbyers to hear.

1836 was the year of the Alamo. Still, in my twenties, this was a very special gig to me as a very young woman growing up in San Antonio knew about the very controversial battle of the Alamo. At its core, the battle of the Alamo was about a group of immigrant settlers fighting for their own free state, their own autonomy, away from the Napoleonic dictatorship of Santa Anna. For me, the story hits close to home. My grandmother, Vadillo, was an immigrant who fled Santa Anna's tyranny, seeking safety and freedom. Her courage her resilience are something I carry with me to this day, and every time I think of her journey, I'm reminded of the strength it takes to fight for what you believe in.

Nuclear Angel

"All of Man's Wisdom is a Foolish Mess"

oil & collage

36X24

NUCLEAR ANGEL

There's at least two sides to this coin

The real issues her halo of flowers above her head

We are blessed with life and love for humanity.

And respecting the power of the nuclear.

An angel contemplating humanity and love.

How do we find the peace,

How do we protect ourselves?

All of the precious environment is at stake

Our responsibility should not be diminished

We are still learning ways of discovering power.

And how can we diminish this radiation

how much radiation poisoning has been admitted already,

And begs the question

Can we control it?

This is about humanity.

HOUSTON

What can I say about Houston? Oh, Houston, you were a city like no other, a place that both nurtured and challenged me, teaching me more than I could have imagined. You were like a stern father and a patient mother, from whom I learned countless life lessons—some beautiful, others hard as steel. It wasn't just the streets I walked or the people I met; it was the way life knocked me down and then taught me how to stand back up.

I fled to Houston, hoping to escape the toxic hold of a boyfriend who was, sadly, consumed by alcohol. His drinking started early in the day—by 11 o'clock, he'd already crossed the line into a world where reason no longer existed. He became someone I didn't recognize—angry, abusive, and out of control. I tried to leave, tried to break free, but no matter how far I ran, somehow, he always found me. Looking back, I wonder if part of me allowed it, still holding on to the love I thought we shared. Maybe my subconscious wanted it that way. I really did love him with all my heart, but he was so bad and unhealthy for my survival. Did I mention somehow, he would always find me and charm his way back into my life. Case in point, I will not mention his name, I'll call him the "Krazy Krow."

It wasn't until I met the 'Krazy Krow' that I truly understood the devastating grip of alcoholism. The name suited him—he could be wild, unpredictable, and chaotic. And yet, despite everything, I can't help but still hold a special place in my heart for him. When he wasn't drinking, he was a different person—exciting, charismatic, full of life. He was one of the most talented jazz trumpet players I'd ever known, with a charm that could light up a room. But that charm vanished the moment the alcohol took over. He also opened my mind to jazz, real jazz, like the classic Miles Davis, John Coltrane, Julian Edwin"Cannonball" Adderly, Dizzy

Gillespie, Charlie Parker, Duke Ellington, and so many more. He would tell me to listen to the horn solos and imitate them. It was a challenge, but, I tried my best, and that's what I loved, scat sing.

But for all the beauty that jazz brought into our lives, there was one thing he loved even more—getting drunk. Krowly drank like a man possessed. It started early—his day would begin with a large glass of orange juice and vodka, and from there, it was a downward spiral. At first, everything seemed fine. He'd laugh, joke, and talk about music, but once he crossed that invisible line, he transformed. It was like watching Dr. Jekyll become Mr. Hyde—a sudden, frightening shift that left no trace of the man I cared for. He could be so cruel, both verbally and physically. This has always been so hard to talk about, even more so to write about.

It took me years for me to leave, to stay away from him. I had become the enabler and was also becoming an alcoholic. We had shared so much music, especially the jazz. This is one of the reasons for leaving San Antonio for Houston.

In my mind, Houston was about one thing—furthering my career. I had no plans to fall into another relationship, no desire to become someone's girlfriend or wife. But life has a funny way of pulling you into the very things you try to avoid. Before I knew it, I found myself walking down paths I hadn't intended, following my heart even when it led me in the wrong direction. It's strange how quickly you can lose yourself, how easily you become 'someone's someone' without even realizing it. Some musician, in my case, had become your boyfriend. It's funny how most men, not all, find themselves backing off because now you "belong" to someone. I never wanted to be an object that belonged to somebody else. So, you find yourself alone and unable to even sit in with another band, because most of them are all friends and didn't want to offend your "boyfriend."

As I look back on this self-destructive situation, I now realized that my confidence and self-esteem were lacking. My sister "Augie" helped me tremendously, as she counseled me to leave him and sent me every self-aid, self-love book that were available, "How to Leave Someone You Think You Love" or was it "How to Leave a Toxic Relationship" by Dianna Thompson and "The Art of Loving" by Eric Fromm, etc.

I had to learn the hard way and couldn't get a gig. The club owners would tell me that he would come to the gig drunk, bring his vile of liquor, which would close the club down, and he'd always cause a scene.

As I slowly learned to love myself again, the decision to leave him became clear. It was hard—heart-wrenching even—but it was necessary. Walking away was one thing, but the real challenge came in the days, weeks, and months after when I had to resist the pull to let him back in. It took time, but eventually, I realized that for my own survival for my own happiness, I could never allow him back into my life. The hardest lesson I learned was that some doors, once closed, need to stay that way. Walk, walk, walk away as soon as possible and as far away as possible. Do not collect two hundred dollars, do not pass go, and whatever you do, "Don't look back."

I understand why women stay with their abuser because I was one.

LAS VEGAS

Funny story: In Las Vegas, I was singing with Doug as a duo. He was a pretty good, okay piano player. At one point, we were booked for a gig in Amarillo, Texas, and somehow managed to leave a week early, thinking our time there was up. Honestly, I wasn't too disappointed. Singing jazz in a country-western bar was pure torture—it felt like trying to fit a square peg in a round hole. The audience wanted twangy guitars and cowboy boots, and there I was, a jazz singer trying to hold my own in a sea of honky-tonk. Unless you are a musician who makes your money performing gigs you don't like, then you would probably not understand. Before coming back to Houston, we decided to head on up to Las Vegas. It was just a little ways away. I remember the first night we got there. I got so pi-eyed (they give you free drinks) I was talking to a one-armed bandit. But, the next day, we decided to audition for the club right on the corner of the shopping center, "The Copa," not the famous "CopaCabana," but a small, intimate bar where our motel was on, right off of Las Vegas Blvd, we got the gig that night, In fact, we jokingly called ourselves "Down & Out in Las Vegas & Just off the Strip "Oh Happy Day! We were in Vegas and got a gig right away.

We almost lasted a month when another piano player came to see me. He was working at the Tropicana with Louis Prima. Louis Prima is best known for his song "Just a Gigolo." He had asked me out and wanted to show me the 'real Vegas' night scene, the scene where the musicians go, the musicians union after-hours club.

When we returned to the apartment that Doug and I shared, he had been drinking a bottle of Jack Daniels. 5'oclack in the morning, Doug comes in with a 57 Magnum. He shot two shots into the ceiling, then lowered his gun and pointed it at Salvatore. If I can remember, I believe that was his name. We were both asleep, but the sound of the gunshots got me up so fast, and as I heard the last gunshot, I saw Doug pointing the gun at me and my date. I jumped out of bed, walked up to him, slapped his face, and said, "What the hell are you doing?" Salvatore kept reminding me that he was holding a loaded gun. He profusely asked Doug's forgiveness, over and over again, as he was putting on his pants, Doug shot above his head, barely missing him. Salvatore barely escaped with his life, barely.

I was shaken to my core. Doug left, and I called my dad and then the police. Of course, they arrested him. Doug hid the gun in the dumpster. (You won't believe this) we still did the gig that night and the weekend. "Somehow, Doug talked me into performing that night. "The show must go on." How do I let myself allow these men to come back into my life and torment me? Fortunately, that was the last time I had a gig with Doug.

Luckily for me, I got a gig singing at the Mint with a Filipino guy who sounded just like Elvis. Also, I found out that many of the agencies in Vegas would only book performers from the Philippines. How do I know this? Because when I called one of these agencies for a booking, he asked me, "What nationality I was." I asked him why that mattered, and he told me, "Because they only book groups from the Philippines." The group I sang with didn't even have a name, but the band members were very cool, including the band leader.

"PAIN"

Gustav Mahler: One of the papers that I wrote for my treatise was about Gustav Mahler. He suffered greatly, as did I at the time. In fact, after my auto accident, I was the passenger, and I suffered from extreme back pain. He writes to his wife: "What is this nonsense about the soul and its sickness?" He suffered from valuator heart disease, brought on by streptococcus, which at that time there was no cure.

"And where should I go to cure it? To find myself in need to be alone. Since I've been seized by this panic, I have been and tried to direct my eyes and ears elsewhere but to rediscover myself, I have got to accept the horrors of loneliness… I have in no sense a hypochondriac's fear of death, as I suppose I have always known that I must die… but, all at once, I have lost the serenity and confidence I had acquired… As far as my work is concerned, it is most depressing to unlearn everything… Unable to work, only at my desk. I need outside exercise for my inner exercises'… after a gentle walk, my pulse beats so fast, and I feel so oppressed that I don't even achieve the desired effect of forgetting my body… This is the greatest calamity I have ever known." Later, he writes,

"Painfully aware

I am becoming 'Body Conscience.'

Aware of every little pain."

Gustav Mahler

1986, I reflect on the time I had a partial hysterectomy, in which I had a near-death experience.

The night that I performed my last gig at the Copa, Mr. Watkins tried to punch me as I walked from the stage to the bathroom. It was the bartender/ manager who followed both myself & Doug and stopped him from hitting me. This was after the night he got drunk and shot up the apartment we were sharing. I thought that we were just friends who shared a common interest: the gig. I proceeded to get drunk, and a military guy picked me up at the bar, accompanied me to my apartment, also raped me the following morning. Yes, I was an idiot to allow this misfortune to happen. Why do we do this to ourselves? I didn't know it at the time, but I had became pregnant.

At the time, I was singing at the Mint Casino downtown La Vegas. I was lucky enough to get a gig with this group. Into the third week, when a piano player wanted to talk to me about singing with him at a piano bar. But, when he took me out to eat, I was unable to concentrate due to too much pain. I asked him to please take me back to my apartment. At the apartment, the pain got worse. I asked one of the neighbors if he had anything for pain. I took two Co-Tylenol 4s, but my pain still got worse. Finally, I knew I had to go to the hospital. I did not know it at the time, but I was having an ectopic pregnancy in which the fallopian tube burst. When I got to the hospital that night, I waited forever for the doctor to see me. Dr. Florence Livingston was my savior, along with Dr. Singer, my anesthesiologist. They let me know that it is a good possibility that I was going to die (it's the law; they have to let you know). We still needed an anesthesiologist to come. Dr. Singer. I remember having an out-of-body experience. I became numb and was watching myself encounter this pain and experience. I found out later that they cannot proceed to operate until the anesthesiologist gives the ok. As we were proceeding, I mentioned to Dr. Singer that I was a singer too. I wrote a song about him entitled "The Singer." It's funny how one remembers situations like this. Dr. Florence Livingston and Dr. Singer, thank you for saving my life.

THE SINGER

(This is the name of my anesthesiologist, Dr. Singer, Las Vegas, a near-death experience from an ectopic pregnancy).

Looking out from my primrose color shades

Saw my reflection in a looking glass

Heard voices calling from across the room

Fell from a tenth-story building in my gloom

The Singer smiled and said,

"Baby, it's much too soon."

Cause if you can put out a breath

You can put out a song

Don't let anyone tell you wrong

The Singer smiled and said,

"Sing your song."

Yes, it was the singer ooh.

Yes, it was the singer,

He kept me from going under.

I remember a time when I thought to myself, 'My greatest ambition is to be a philanthropist.' It wasn't about fame or recognition—it was about giving back in the most meaningful way I could imagine. I dreamed of building a wing in honor of the incredible doctors who saved my life, a tangible way to show my gratitude for the care and compassion that kept me alive when I needed it most. I wanted to give others the same chance, the same hope.

Thank goodness that abortion and women still had rights, and medical help for those who suffered complications was still the law of the land to save them and keep them from dying or bleeding out.

I am alive!

TERRIFIED

This isn't the kind of terror that comes from a horror movie or a gripping mystery novel. No, it's much more real, much more personal. It's the kind of terror that grips you when you're facing a spinal stenosis operation, a laminectomy on L4 and L5. I told myself—and others—'I'm going to be strong, everything will be alright. I'll face whatever comes my way and come out triumphant.' But deep down, the fear lingered, whispering doubts in the quiet moments. My girlfriend went in for colon cancer last year. Each time she got chemotherapy, she got worse. Her resistance became nil, and finally, because her resistance was so low, she got Covid and died.

Again, I tried to reassure myself—'I'm strong. I can handle whatever comes my way. Everything will be alright.' But in truth, the future felt uncertain, abstract, almost too absolute. What if I got COVID? 'Stupid COVID,' I thought bitterly. It was still lurking, especially in hospitals where my surgery would take place. And then there was the risk of the surgery itself—what if something went wrong? 'Complications,' the word hung in the air like a shadow.

I do trust my surgeons. Dr. Webb, my back surgeon, and Dr. Bowser, my vascular surgeon, explained that it would take up to six months for the internal sutures to scare and heal and a year for my laminectomy to completely heal.

Well, there goes another lost year.

Yes, I believe everything will be Okay, it will be alright. I think.

But, in truth,

I was TERRIFIED!

This last laminectomy on L4-L5 was something far beyond pain. It wasn't just physical discomfort—it was what I can only describe as 'evil pain,' the kind that clings to your soul and refuses to let go. For three long months, I lived in that agony, a torment that felt like it would never end.

At first, it was depressing, and I cried a lot. Now, I'm just numb and live with chronic pain. Complication, yes, there were complications. Three months later, after my laminectomy, a fluid buildup inside me, and they had to operate on me again. And so, I kept going because what else could I do? Now, I find myself in a state of acceptance, just dealing with the chronic pain as best as I can. But I survived. Through it all, I'm still here, and that's something. The pain has given me time—time to reflect, to think about what matters most, and to recognize my own resilience in ways I never had before.

This wasn't just pain—it was 'Evil Pain,' a kind of suffering that digs deep into your bones and makes you cry out in the night, night after night. For two long months, I cried myself to sleep, the weight of it pressing down on me like a relentless force. It was pain that felt like it had no end, no escape.

LAMINECTOMY

Is a type of surgery in which a surgeon removes part or all of the vertebral bone (lamina). Failed back syndrome or post-laminectomy syndrome is a condition characterized by chronic pain following back surgeries… Common symptoms associated with FBS include diffuse, dull, and aching pain involving the back or legs. Abnormal sensibility may include sharp, pricking, and stabbing pain in the extremities. The term "post-laminectomy syndrome" is used to indicate the same condition as failed back syndrome."

Wikipedia Google

'Pain'—it's a word that can seem so simple, but for those of us who've lived it, it's far more complex. I know pain intimately—physical, mental, and emotional. I've walked through the fire, endured its scorching flames, and somehow, I've come out the other side. But the scars remain, reminders of the battles fought both within and without.

The physical pain is the obvious of all pains, but what makes a person, a man or woman, think that it's okay to hit, pull hair, punch, spit on, drag, beat, and even strangle another person? To call her names belittle her till her confidence is lost in the brutality of a Drunken Narcissist. I often think about men who see women not as people but as objects—things to be used, discarded, and broken until there's nothing left but an empty shell. These are memories I wish I could forget, but they are part of my story. 'For the grace of God, go I,' I remind myself. Somehow, I survived. I lived through it all, even when it felt like I wouldn't.

But, I remember being there, vulnerable and unable to defend yourself. I thank God, the gods, Allah, the Universe, "She" that my angels or my ancestors protected me from this kind of evil. And finally, I had the sense to leave.

MY FATHER

Perhaps it all started with my father. I can't shake the memory of that day—him towering over me, his fist landing on my face over and over again. The impact of each blow felt like it echoed into eternity. I was just a child, and it was the day before I was supposed to start 6th grade, a day that should have been filled with excitement and hope for the future. Instead, it became a day etched in pain. Thank goodness for the Theresian nuns who took me under their wing, I attribute myself esteem and all that is good and pure in heart to these most excellent humans. Who Taught me how to think, taught me to love humanity, but especially taught me how to love myself and to love others.

But, in many ways, the most painful abuse wasn't physical—it was the verbal assaults from someone I loved, or at least someone I thought loved me. Words have a way of cutting deeper than any fist, leaving wounds that linger long after the moment has passed.

My sister, "Augie," who gave me all those self-love books, made me realize that I did not love myself. It's funny, but one doesn't attribute love to self. It was an awakening to learn that I really did not love myself. It begs the question, "Why?" And again, it goes back to my father, who beat my mother on a regular basis.

When you grow up in an environment where 'machismo' is the norm, you start to believe that hitting and verbal abuse are just part of love. It warps your understanding of what love is supposed to be. But eventually, I had to unlearn those lessons, to realize that real love does NOT hit, and it certainly doesn't belittle or tear you down. Love is supposed to lift you up, not leave you bruised and broken. And as much as I loved and still love my father, it took me forever to unlearn what a lot of women suffer. Most of the men I dated or were my partners were abusive. Central

Catholic High School, Bro. R. Martins abused me in a way that I did not know that his control over me hurt more than those who hit or abused me verbally. I made the mistake of telling him everything about my life. Of course, he was my mentor. But, my first year of college, I told him that I slept with a guy who didn't even have sex. Believe it or not, I was still a virgin then. He replied, "I don't want anything to do with you ever again." It was as though someone had pulled the rug out from underneath me. I was in a perpetual fall. I felt worthless dirty, as though "Who could ever love me?" My counselor and my sister helped me to realize that he was grooming me all those years for his own ego. It took me years to learn to love myself, and I promised myself that no one would ever abuse me like that again, not physically mentally. emotionally or even spiritually.

My ex-husband, whom I won't name, let's just call him, the "Gooch."

Gave me two things: grief and a venereal disease. We were only together as man and wife for a year. I ask myself why did I marry this (pause) "Gooch" Why? I realized that I was pregnant and good Catholic girls always marry the person who got them pregnant. Peter Yarrow from the "Peter, Paul, and Mary" folk singers sang at my wedding in Kerrville, Texas. I was also one of the featured artists that year. My father was crying. I think it was for the fact that he didn't want

me to marry this "Gooch." On our way to Nashville, Tennessee, the Gooch wanted to see his mother, he was peeved at me because I had ruined his vacation. I was so pregnant at the time and, throwing up and just feeling miserable. Funny thing, the "Gooch" was a marriage counselor. I was his third X-wife. He had asked me from the beginning to have an abortion. But as a good Catholic, I chose not to have this abortion until he gave me an ultimatum. "Have an abortion, or I'll just leave you." I did. I did have that abortion and thought I was going to die. I was almost at my trimester. When I was finally allowed to leave the clinic, as I walked out, he had a smile on his face and asked," How was it?" I replied, "I don't want to talk about it." Then he came back with, "Everybody that comes out of this operation has a smile on their face, and you look like you've just seen death." His exact words. I ran back to the room where the counselor was and cried. She was a great comfort. I ran to the elevator, went down to street level, crossed the street, and hid in the IHOP to call my dad. The "Gooch" finally found me and let me know that he will take me back to San Antonio and leave me there with my father. We were divorced that same year... To say the least, marrying the "Gooch" was a BIG Mistake. And by the way, I am now pro-choice. A woman's body should only be governed by no one else but herself.

There is another type of pain, a spiritual and psychological pain.

THE INTERNATIONAL BIBLE COLLEGE

Becoming Pentecostal
Normalcy, God is Bigger Than Hallelujah Hill

When I returned from Los Angeles, I found myself once again singing along the beautiful San Antonio River Walk, this time at the '1836 Restaurant,' a fantastic BBQ joint that quickly became my home. I spent three wonderful years there, sharing my voice with the river and its passersby. When new owners took over and changed the name to 'Casey's On The River,' I continued to sing there for another two years. Those years are filled with so many cherished memories. Each note I sang intertwined with the laughter and stories of the people who gathered there. My dear friend, Jon Roland, made it a point to come every night I sang, from Tuesday through Saturday, and indulge in all the delicious meats the restaurant had to offer. We developed a deep friendship during those nights filled with music and laughter. In fact, I was fortunate enough to live in the 'Estrella' mansion, right on the riverwalk, for at least three years; Jon owned it. It was a beautiful place steeped in history, and I felt lucky to call it home.

When I first met Jon, he had heard my voice amplified on the river, and like a siren, he followed the voice and came in to meet me. He also asked if I would sing at his mother's funeral. Of course, I said "yes." We immediately became the best of friends. Jon Drew Roland was a steadfast presence in my life, always there through both the good times and the bad. A naval officer by training, he carried himself with the grace of a true gentleman. Jon dedicated much of his life to creating 'The Constitution Society' and the 'Constitution.org.' Through his work, he made available a treasure trove of writings and documents from the American Revolution to the present, enriching the public's understanding of our nation's history. Not only did he upload the "Constitution of the United States," the writing of Jefferson, Benjamin Franklin, etc. etc.,. A must-read. It still exist today.

While I was singing at the 1836 club, a restaurant named after the year of the Alamo, I met some Pentecostal ministers who encouraged me to pray for a Bible. With a mixture of skepticism and hope, I did just that. A week later, to my surprise, there it was—waiting at my door. It felt like a sign, a moment of connection to something greater. I also met a girl who had been running away from home because she told me that her dad had sold everything to dedicate his life to his mission. My curiosity eventually led me to a prayer meeting where I met Michael, known as the 'Barefooted Preacher.' At that point in my life, I was deeply immersed in the fervor of the Pentecostal scene, feeling a sense of urgency and passion for my faith. Meeting Michael felt like destiny, as though the universe was guiding me to those who would further awaken my spirit. At the prayer meeting, Michael would pray over the faithful, and I was one. He started to cry intensely, which scared me a little, while he prophesied over me and started to cry. As he prayed over me and quietly said, "The Lord was going to break me and that I was going to go through the fire (metaphorically speaking). Then the Lord would rebuild my spiritual being." That Sunday night, my parents asked if I would see my mother's psychiatrist. It felt like a pivotal moment in my life. In those days, I often turned to my King James Bible for guidance, opening it to any page and pointing my finger down, believing that God was communicating with me through the words I found there. It read, "To obey your parents is pleasing to the Lord." The next morning, we were off to see Dr. Weis. He suggested that they wanted to run test on me. I was told I would have residency at a mental institution called 'Villa Rosa,' and it would only be for three days. Those three days turned into nearly forty, a length of time that felt endless and surreal. About midway, I was broken. They make you take psychotic medication, I call them drugs, and if you refuse, they will, well, you know. It was just like "One Flew Over the Cuckoo's Nest." The building that I was in had no windows, and no one was allowed to see me except my parents. I became one of those patients you see that shuffle. Time lost all meaning in that place. A minute felt like an hour, an hour stretched into a day, and a day seemed to last an eternity. It was a mental nightmare, a spiritual crisis, and I found myself crying almost constantly, each tear a release for the pain I felt inside.

There was a riot of some of the patients who protested how they were treated and especially having to take these psychotic drugs. Time lost all meaning in that place. A minute felt like an hour, an hour stretched into a day, and a day seemed to last an eternity. It was a mental nightmare, a spiritual crisis, and I found myself crying almost constantly, each tear a release for the pain I felt inside. Maybe it was a two days. When I woke, it seemed that this was the end of me, I thought. I thought that they would just keep sending in more doctors my way and would keep me as long as they willed. The other patients whispered that they would only send in more doctors to keep me there for as long as they desired. The idea was chilling, feeding my paranoia and deepening my sense of entrapment. I felt like a pawn in a game I didn't understand. I thought to myself, "They think I'm crazy because I love Jesus." I was just a very young and very zealous Charismatic Christian. They're going to keep me here forever. There's a scripture in the old testament that is written, "Without a vision, my people perish." I felt my whole life slip through my mind. It was then that I wrote a letter to Brother David Coote, the president of the International Bible College. "They think I'm crazy because I love Jesus." It was tear-stained and crumpled. I thought that they would keep the letter or give it to Dr. Weis, and he would keep it for his records. A couple of days later, Brother David Coote came to see me, and of course, they told him that only family was allowed. He replied, "Okay, I'll see you when I come back with Miss Cisneros' lawyers. He would bring me tapes of the student at the bible college tapes of songs to cheer me up. The students at the Bible College were praying for me. He truly was a holy man, so was Bro. Troyer, birds, sparrows would light on him. He had a glow about his body. His aura was one of Godliness. I was a minister in my own right; music was my ministry. It was my way of reaching out to others sharing love and hope. However, when another teacher encouraged me to join a Bluegrass Festival and then street evangelize in New York, I hesitated and ultimately chose not to go. He would preach in class about those who break their word, and I felt the weight of his disappointment pressing down on me. I sought out counsel with Bro. Troyer, "Avoid the appearance of evil' he replied. I thought it was for more than just myself, a school field trip, and decided to stay In San Antonio instead.

God has to be bigger than "Hallelujah Hill,' I thought to myself. My beady brain can't imagine the mind and enormity of God's brain.

As summer rolled in, I secured a job at Harmon's Health Food Store, a fresh start in a new environment. Alongside that, I returned to singing on the San Antonio Riverwalk, my passion reignited, and once again, sharing my music with the world. I thought a lot about God and how he had many names. I realized that I know my Bible, but I really didn't know 'God,' 'Allah,' 'Jehovah,' 'The Great I Am,'" 'The Alpha the Omega," "Dios," "Nature," "the Universe," etc. I even thought maybe animals, the birds have their own god. I thought about crickets and grasshoppers. When they rub their hands together, are they praying? It would be a wonderful prayer, probably for peace and for the earth. I embarked on a journey to understand other philosophies, particularly existential ones. I delved into the works of Khalil Gibran, Herman Hesse's 'Narcissus and Goldman,' 'Demian,' and 'Siddhartha,' along with various existentialist thinkers. Each page I turned opened new avenues of thought, challenging my perspectives and enriching my understanding of life.

So why was I so attracted to these holy and religious people, I guess it was that I was trying to find myself.

I know that I never want to be a fanatic again. But my faith, my spirituality, my beliefs are deep, and I will always cherish the time I spent at the "International Bible College" on "Hallelujah Hill. By the way,

By the way, I identify as a constitutionalist and firmly believe in the principle of 'Separation of Church and State.' It's a belief that reflects my commitment to ensuring that personal faith and public policy remain distinct, allowing for freedom of belief and expression for all.

ACRYLIC ALCOHOL INK PAINTINGS

Milk Thistle Leaves

Acrylic Alcohol Ink

14X11

"NOT ONE BIT"

I do not like being disabled

I do not like it, not one bit.

I do not like being unable

To walk, to run, dance, play, and even have a fit.

Feels like a fish out of water

Only enough for him to breathe

Or a bird whose wings have been clipped

Not able to fly, to soar

Not even able to flip

I do not like being unable

I do not like it

Not one bit

Not ever knowing that I will never

Be able to hang out with my musicians and artist friends

Not to be able to dance and Jazz it up

To drink with all my favorite ladies and gents.

And maybe even eat some chips.

I do not like being unable

To run and play

To stomp around the pool all-day

While listening to music, so cool

Coltrane, Ella, Aretha, Stevie, Dizzy, Miles

And even Steely Dan.

Yes, It's very hard to admit

I do not like being unable, disabled

I do not like it

Not One Bit

Red Poppies on a Yellow Background

Acrylic Alcohol Ink

14X11

THE WAR GAME

What is this madness

Called "Hate"

This insanity

Called "War"

In dreams, obscurities

That brings me close to those I love

Apart from the hustle and bustle

Of the world's sadness

The war games never end

What monsters trying to control another

Oh, sweet immortal lives

Once I dreamt

That I was

Dating Paul McCarthy

But when he left

Because so many people were after him

As he walked away

He kept getting fatter and fatter

Just a dream

I can hear my heart

Whispers and tells me that I am part of you

A sadness befalls

The announcer on CNN

Recalls… Recounts, who dies, who lives

War,

D-evil's playground

D-evil spins

Nobody wins

Blue Flowers on Yellow Background

Acrylic Alcohol Ink

14X11

WHO'D NOTE

Who'd note it would be love
You'd never convince me
Who'd note it would be you
Our love would last longer
Who'd note I'd still be here with you? Love

You know it would be over.
Cause you found a lover.
You don't need to be mean to me
I'm not so blind
That I can't see
Wanna be with you
Always, Forever

It's my heart, dear
That's bringing it down to you
I wanna tell you
I'm bringing it home to you
Who'd note It would be love
Wanna be with you always
Forever.

(Based on a Fm Blues)

Cats in the Garden

Acrylic Alcohol Ink

14X11

THOUGHT FOR TODAY

We don't see ultraviolet rays

Insects do.

Maybe God is color-blind.

Or maybe God is multi-colored.

He must have had a moment when

He created man

As He choose their features

Choose their color

Choosing them with love, affection & even humor.

How wonderful that the world is

Multi-colored.

Otherwise, it would

Be so

So very boring.

Hearts & Flowers

Acrylic Alcohol Ink

Collage

ON THE CORNER OF WAVERLY & PEACOCK STREET

It's hot here on the corner of Waverly & Peacock Street

The sky washed with ultramarine blue and lavender

Where hardly a whisper, a furl, a curl of barely

a cloud passes by.

I saw two yellow butterflies enthralled in a dance

Against the sunlit sky

Entranced amid the traffic, zooming by

A child plays by her grandfather's side

tricycle she rides, she's ready to fly

"They have rockets and missiles," someone cries,"

And on the surface, ground zero, there is no purpose,

Not even a rhyme.

The plumed serpent arises,

"Target you, target me, target thee."

Not so very far away, someone sighs,

"INNOCENCE NEEDS NO DEFENSE"

Today, I saw two butterflies enthralled in a dance.

Life goes on here on the corner of Waverly and Peacock Street

Where hardly a whisper, a furl, a curl

Of barely a cloud passes by.

Red Flowers Fallin' in Water

Acrylic Alcohol Ink

14X11

124

DONNA'S WORLD PEACE AND UNITY SONG

(a soldier's lament)

It rained rainbows on me today

It rained ribbons of peace

Ribbons of light gently kissed my eyes

Rivers of peace from your smile.

Streams of desire, my heart lights on fire

Music is in me, It's only the beginning

It rained rainbows of peace today

You left me standing in a shower of kindness

Lightning filled your eyes. Tears filled mine

Not for sadness but for joy

You lifted me, and you gave me life

The gift of life you gave me

It brought me to my knees, facing eternity

The treasure of death

The soil that made me

Earth's sweet, fragrant breath,

Sweet, fragrant, pungent earth, I'm Listening

It rained rainbows on me today

It rained ribbons of peace

Prisms of light gently kissed my eyes

Like sculptured smoke rings

I keep your memory in my mind

You showered your love on me today

You kissed my lips and took my breath away

You showered your love light

And left me wondering why

You went away?

I Am Jazz

Acrylic Alcohol Ink

Collage

11X14

GHETTO-LICIOUS

When your living with a jazz musician

and resident Hippie,

And you're feeling Ghetto Fabulous

Think about this

The human being is a wonderful thing,

Although I still put the creatures of the earth and sea

above you and me

And there is something

Miraculous about being alive

Sometimes, it fills me with so much pride.

I'm feeling Ghetto-Licious,

Ghetto-fabulous

You gotta play it with love

And that comes from inside.

Red & Yellow Flowers

Acrylic Alcohol Ink

11X14

DON'T LET IT GET YOU DOWN

Winds swept in from the north

The breeze carried with it one refrain

"Life is what you make it. You know you just can't fake it."

It keeps whispering that sweet refrain

"Don't let it get you down

Don't let trouble stand in your way

Your problems are as small or as big as you let them

So, don't let them get you down."

Oh, there's Jon Roland smiling back at me. He keeps saying, "Let it be."

The challenge of it all sweeps me off my feet

It keeps coming like a tidal wave

Just like the winds of yesterday,

My friends keep calling out my name

They know of a power that lies within this hour

It keeps whispering that sweet refrain

Don't let it get you down

Don't let trouble stand in your way

You're problems are as small or as big as you let them

So, don't let them get you down

The wisdom of your soul keeps reaching to me

My heart is filled with sympathy

There was a man named Jesus; He sacrificed for me

You know my heart was filled with grief

Like mirrors of my soul, I see

My eyes are filled with tears for you and me

My heart cries out for truth,

My life was meant for me, and you

Don't let it get you down

Don't let trouble stand in your way

Your problems are as small or as big as you let them

So Don't let it get you down.

Violets

Acrylic Alcohol Ink

FALLING

(a tribute to the heroes, victims, and first responder of 911)

I heard about your sons and daughters

About your mother and your father, too

So early in the morning

I thought I saw you through the traffic lights

It was on the news

You were falling

I saw you falling from the heavens Like frozen butterfly wings assailed with anguish relief.

There were scarves and jewelry, too

So many color, so many hue

Shoes, Red, White, and Blue

They were falling

Falling from the heavens

Falling from the skies

Into God's hands

Into his precious lullaby

I thought I heard the angels singing

I thought I heard them cry

When you were calling to say

"I love you."

Calling to say "Goodbye'

You were falling

Clouds of darkness Chased humanity

Relics of heroes

Silenced by time with unrelenting grief

They were falling

They were falling

They were falling.

MY JAZZ WORLD

As a proud member of the Southwest Texas University Jazz Band—now known as Texas State University—I had the honor of being a featured vocalist for the prestigious Hondo Award. I also received the Down Beat Award for my work as a jazz vocalist with an ensemble. These achievements were more than accolades; they were affirmations of my passion and commitment to the jazz world.

My interest in jazz ignited at the tender age of seventeen when I began performing for several consecutive years along the San Antonio River Walk. I graced various clubs and restaurants with my music, each performance weaving me deeper into the vibrant fabric of the jazz scene. It was my guitar teacher Jesse Hernandez that turned me on to Ella Fitzgerald, also to Lead Belly, BB King, Miles Davis, Cleo Lane, Billie Holiday, Sarah Vaughan, Nina Simone, Dizzy Gillespie, and many, many more. I learned that there were many genres of jazz, and I loved them all, but especially scat singing. I didn't care that I was a good scat singer at the beginning. I just knew that's what I wanted to do.

Then, I met Jay Fort, who was such a great influence on my music. When asked if he would help me with my music and played my songs for him, he was more than helpful, teaching me how to understand the mechanics of form and what music scales went with what chords, as well as chord progressions and how to sing not only 'inside' but also, to sing 'outside' the chord changes. I immersed myself in the world of jazz, fervently dedicating myself to listening to as many jazz singers and musicians as I could find. Each note, each phrase became a lesson, a chance to absorb the artistry and innovation that jazz had to offer.

HOME WITH FAMILY & FRIENDS

The most important chapter of my life is my family and friends. There's so much to say about my family, but I will try to synapse the importance of growing up with such a dysfunctional family, whom I love dearly. My mother was diagnosed with manic-depressive schizophrenia, a heavy burden to bear. Considering all that she endured, it's nothing short of miraculous that she managed to find some semblance of happiness amidst the turmoil. It was a time Tacoma, Washington, when they gave certain medication freely for her post-pregnancy depression. Drugs that are now banned in the United States are lithium, Thioridazine, and other antipsychotic medications. They also gave her shock treatments. I remember one time she told me that after they had given her these shock treatments, that she saw angels going up and down a ladder. I believe they were ministering to her. When she told the doctors about her visions, instead of reassurance, they opted to give her more shock treatments. It's a tragic reminder of how often the mental health system failed those who needed help the most. Life can be so cruel even if it is well-meaning. She was never the same. When we eventually moved back to San Antonio, the weight of her struggles became too much for her to bear, and she ended her life at a tragically young age—in her forties. The loss was devastating, leaving an indelible mark on my heart. She was on suicide watch at the Villa Rosa Mental Hospital, where she hung herself. The week before she died, Mom told me that Grandma Vadillo, her mother, would frequently visit her. My grandma, 'Tita,' had been dead for over ten years. I will always remember my mother as one of the most beautiful women I ever knew. She loved her children fiercely, as well as her husband. My siblings and I, Tony and Augie, experienced a somewhat normal childhood filled with laughter and mischief—at least until the darker clouds of our family life would creep in. Those moments of light felt like precious gems amidst the chaos. My little brother, Steven, was born ten years later. He has recently disappeared into the abyss. My only hope is that he is happy, safe, and loved.

My father was a walking dichotomy. On one hand, my love for him felt endless; on the other, I grappled with the hatred for the abuse he inflicted on both my mother and myself. It was a tumultuous relationship, defined by conflicting emotions that I still wrestle with today.

The Rain Forest Lament

UPC/EAN

194171752995

THE PAUL HINDEMITH FOUNDATION

Texas Mysterium for Modern Composers

Blonay, Switzerland

1994

DR. RUSSELL REIPE

It wasn't until I was accepted at Southwest Texas State University—now known as Texas State University, San Marcos—that I truly began to understand the art of musical development and the intricacies of composition under the guidance of my mentor and greatest teacher, Dr. Russell Reipe. I felt both privileged and blessed to have Dr. Reipe as my teacher; he was a direct legacy of the extraordinary Nadia Boulanger, the renowned French composer, conductor, and teacher who revolutionized music in the early 20th century. Among her illustrious students were icons like Aaron Copland, Quincy Jones, Philip Glass, and countless others, each a testament to her profound influence on the world of music.

TEXAS MYSTERIUM FOR MODERN COMPOSERS

European Tour

June 9 - 21, 1994

"The Texas Mysterium for Modern Composers." Blonay, Switzerland, the Hindemith Foundation had never invited a University from the United States. We were the first to set a president for Southwest Texas State University. Where we featured our composition "Rain Forest Lament," co-composed by Jay Fort M.M. and myself. Realized in the electronic recording studio, this electronic composition accompanied a jazz chamber ensemble featuring Dr. James Polk on piano, Michael Wurst on jazz viola, Al Gomez on trumpet, Eva Baumgarten on alto Saxophone, Jay Fort, Tenor Sax, Jay Rosen on Tuba and myself, vocalist. Rain Forest Lament is a lamentation of the death and destruction of the Rain Forest.

We were also honored to be invited to perform at prestigious venues such as the Dukes Jazz Club in Montreux, Switzerland; Beethoven Hall at the Conservatory of Innsbruck in Austria; and The Triebhaus in Lenk, Germany, among others. Each performance was a unique opportunity to share our music and message with diverse audiences.

The initial inspiration for a time-sequenced composition using a variety of instruments and computerized Soundscape came from the idea of saving our planet and our wonderful rainforest. The rainforests are the lungs of our world, facing relentless destruction and devastation. Through diverse instrumentation and the crafted soundscape, we aimed to evoke the rich sounds of the forest—the calls of birds, the trumpeting of elephants, and the enchanting chorus of insects. Each element was carefully chosen to immerse the listener in the vibrant life of the rainforest. The Soundscape was written and recorded on synthesizers, realized in the electronic studio. With that done, the piece encompassed form and improvisation.

The Soundscape is a reminder of the (part A) "The Beauty of the Rain Forest" and (part B) "The Beast Who Destroys," a reminder of the relentless greed of man. Throughout this composition, the opportunity to improvise as a group or soloist can become aleatoric. The musicians have the freedom to improvise not only as soloists but also within the tutti sections, creating a dynamic interplay that embodies the concept of entropy in music. This allows for moments of chaos and beauty to coexist.

The composers wish to convey a constant duality consisting of two opposing elements: life and death, pristine serenity to dark, foreboding evil, the electronic tape vs. the chamber ensemble, or the Soundscape of synthetic and industrial noise pollution vs. the beauty of acoustic, organic and earthy ambiance of the ensemble; in other words the *"beauty of the rainforest"* vs. *"the beast who destroys."*

There are three ingredients that give *Rain Forest* its unified cohesiveness. 1.) the conductor (who is the catalyst and gives this composition it's structure), 2.) the performers and the vocalist (a siren of the forest), and 3.) the electronic tape (which is the backbone). Within the composition, numerous elements of symbolism arise in relation to the sounds of the rainforest, reflecting the intricate stratification and layering of musical statements. Each layer represents a facet of the ecosystem, contributing to a greater understanding of its complexity. Polyphonic (or polyphonous) devices are used in which more than one theme is played at one time or individually. The treatment of these simultaneities and their independent parts, along with the use of poignant motivic developments, weaves throughout both movements, A and B, creating a seamless connection between the thematic elements.

It is not only the United States but also those abroad whose pernicious attitude of greed are destroying the rainforest and increasing the rate of deforestation at an ever-increasing rate. We often operate under the illusion of human perfection, believing ourselves to be limitless in energy and driven solely by self-interest, yet we continually cry out for 'more.' This raises an essential question: 'Are we the beauty-makers or the beasts who destroy?' It is a poignant reflection on our dual nature. It is the composers' deepest wish to convey through both sound and prose the feelings that weigh heavily on our hearts—a 'Lament' for something precious, evanescent, and irreplaceable. This work serves as a reminder of what we stand to lose and the urgency of preserving our planet.

Rain Forest Lament

"To Save the Rain Forest is to Save Ourselves"
Composed by: Carol "Csi" Cisneros & Jay T. Fort c. 1994

"LAMENTO POR LOS BOSQUES DE LLUVIA"

"Lamento Por Los Bosqus de Lluvia"

La guerradura de la verdad

Se dejan ver mediante los ojos

Hichados y lleno de lagrimas

Estamos matando los Bosques de lluvia

Ya no existe' los bosques de lluvia

El Senor, protégé los bosques de lluvia

"TO SAVE THE RAIN FOREST IS TO SAVE OURSELVES"

"Rain Forest Lament," co-composed by Carol Cisneros M.M. and Jay Fort M.M., was created to bring awareness facing mankind (an existential threat) when we violate our environment and strip the rain forest of its' protective mantel, the retention of soil which helps protect the forest from erosion, regeneration becomes virtually impossible. Deforestation leads to desertification, this burns fossil fuels, creating a "greenhouse effect" where the hole in the ozone layer increases. "Air temperature is influenced by the proportion between incoming radiation from the sun and outgoing radiation from the earth into space," creating more forest fires in urban areas and will burn at an ever-increasing rate. To disregard this balance regarding the patterns of the rainfall leads to an increase of carbon dioxide, creating desertification. CO_2 becomes extremely concentrated. Less heat is radiated back into space. Creating higher sea levels, a "Greenhouse Effect' or Global Warming. Marus Jacobs, *"Tropical RainForest, A First Encounter,"*

"Are we the Beauty Makers

Or the Beast who destroys?"

RAIN FOREST LAMENT

We are beguiled by life's mysteries

Brought into this world by birth

The war of our existence

The struggle for life

Are we the instruments

By which we inherited this wondrous earth?

Or the beast of greed

whose end is destruction?

We are killing our mother, the earth

And now there exist no more the wonders of God's creation.

Oh God, protect our mother and all that she has to offer

Protect this gem, this beautiful blue & green planet.

There are fires everywhere

And now there is no more water

What of man,

What of the birds & the beast

What of our family & friends

What of the bees? the buzzing of bees

What a beautiful sound

What of the birds chirping?

What beautiful melodies

laughter and sighs

What of our children

We are the Beauty Makers

But we can become

The instruments of death & destruction

Let us choose life.

ALBEDO, GLOBAL WARMING AND THE GREENHOUSE EFFECT

Albedo is the process of measuring the earth's surface to reflect heat/radiation back into space. White reflects, and black absorbs. The polar caps reflect heat/radiation back into space, yet because of global warming, the polar caps are melting. Hence, less heat/radiation is reflected back into space. "Albedo is the fraction of solar energy (shortwave radiation) reflected from Earth back to space. It is the measure of the reflectivity of the earth's surface. Ice snow has high albedo, bouncing most of the sunlight back into space. + – www.esr.olrg/outreach/glossary/albedo.htm

The loss of Arctic ice is of particular concern. The ice is disappearing quite fast; not only is albedo decreasing, but the loss triggers a positive feedback. By exposing the ocean's surface to sunlight, the water warms up. This melts the ice from underneath while man-made CO_2 in the atmosphere warms the surface. Humidity also increases; water vapor is a powerful greenhouse gas. More ice, therefore, melts, which exposes more water, which melts more ice from underneath… This loop fuels itself, the effect getting more and more pronounced." –www.skepticalscience.com/earth-albedo-effect.htm "The greenhouse effect is the process by which absorption and emission of infrared radiation by gasses in a planet's atmosphere warm its lower atmosphere and surface… Human activity since the Industrial Revolution has increased the amount of greenhouse gasses in the atmosphere, leading to increased radiative forcing from CO_2, methane, tropospheric ozone, CFCs, and nitrous oxide.– Spahni, Renato; et al. (November 2006) "Atmospheric Methane and Nitrous Oxide of the late Pleistocene from Antarctic Ice Cores." –Science 310 "Global dimming, a gradual reduction in the amount of global direct irradiance at the Earth's surface, was observed from 1961 until at least 1990. The main cause of this dimming is particulates produced by volcanoes and human-made pollutants, which exerts a cooling effect by increasing the reflection of incoming sunlight. The effects of the products of fossil fuel combustion –CO_2 and aerosols – have partially offset one another in recent decades... Black carbon is second only to carbon dioxide for its contribution to global warming... Sulfates act as cloud absorbing solar radiation. Particulates have an indirect effect... Soot directly absorbs solar radiation, which heats the atmosphere and cools the surface. High soot, such as rural India, as much as 50% of surface warming due to greenhouse gasses may be masked by atmospheric brown clouds.... When deposited, especially on glaciers or on ice in arctic regions, the lower surface Albedo can also directly heat the surface. The influences of particulates, including black carbon, are most pronounced in the tropics and sub-tropics, particularly in Asia, while the effects of greenhouse gasses are dominant in the extratropics and southern hemisphere." – www.Wikipedia.org

THE SCORE!

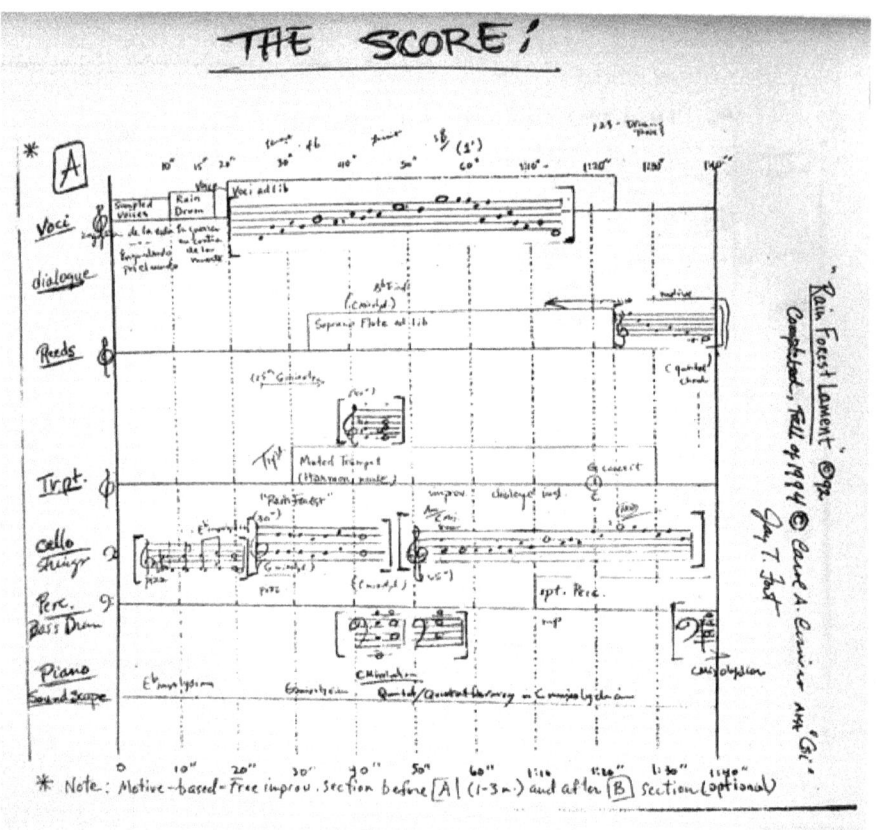

Rain Forest Lament

The Score Part A

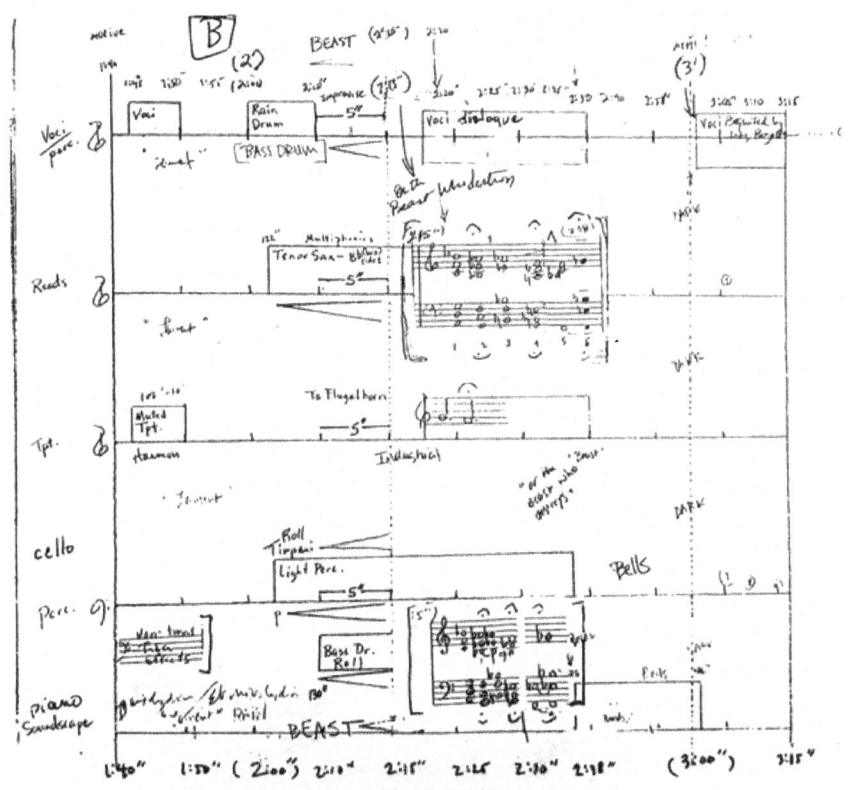

Rain Forest Lament

Score, Part B

"Or the Beast, Who Destroys"

NOTES FROM RAIN FOREST LAMENT

Composer(s) → Carol "Csi" Cisneros,
Jay T. Fort.

Southwest Texas State University
Composition completed — Fall 1994 —
Firestation studio,
San Marcos, Tx.

Bobby Arnold → Engineer
Roger Williams → Engineer / Elect. Tape

Tape = 9'20"
Completed Composition = approx. 13'.

✗ Motive-based Improv Section before [A] and
after end of [B].

"Remember, O Lord, what is come upon us:
Consider and behold our reproach…
We have drunken our water for money
and our wood is sold unto us
for money."
Lamentations 5:1-4

The Rights of Our Planet

a ballet

The Rights of Our Planet (a ballet) is a composition that embraces the concept of aleatoric improvisation, reflecting a deeper understanding of humanity's communal awareness of our environment and our responsibilities to all living beings. At its core, the issue is Human Rights—the quality of life we strive for. Our true enemy is not one another; it is prejudice, war, hatred, and ignorance that divide us from our rightful inheritance and all that the Earth has to offer. In this dance, we recognize that animals too, partake in this celebration of life, and with this realization, we embrace our world as a shared creation, acknowledging all creatures as our brothers and sisters as we dance the joyful gigue of life.

The Rights of Our Planet
a ballet.

Stage Ensemble – order of Players

Stage for Dancers & Performers

dancers placed throughout audience
and front of stage.

The Rights of Our Planet, a ballet is a composition, which is partially aleatoric. Based on a a better understanding of man's communal awareness to his enviroment and his responsibilities to all living things. We must recognize that our enemy is not man and that prejudism, war, hatreds, and ignorance are what seperates us from our ... inheretance, the earth and all that she has to offer. The issue is Human Rights, and the quality in which we live them. Animals do dance and with this thought we embrace our world of creation as our brothers, and dance the gigve of life.

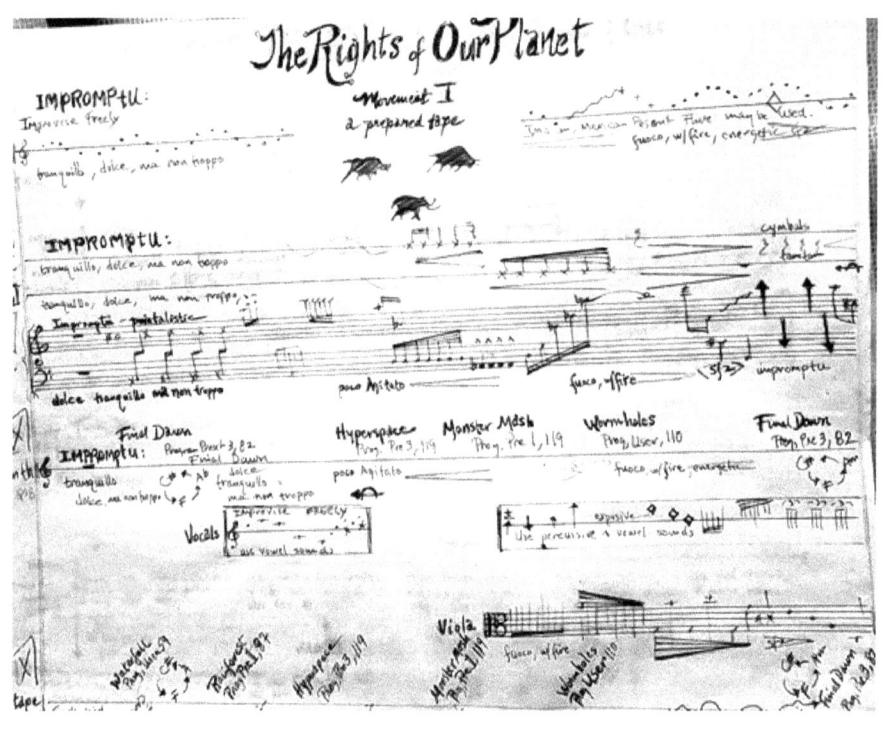

The Rights of Our Planet

Con Mis Hermanos de Alma
Movement III.

The Rights of Our Planet

The final movement, "Perpetual Peace," features a recorded electronic soundscape, realized in the electronic studio at Southwest Texas State University. This recorded music, composed in the style of musique concrète, serves as a backdrop for a Jazz Chamber Ensemble. This movement is characterized by pure aleatoric elements, where players interact intermittently, responding to one another and to the music in real-time. It invites any musicians who wish to join in, including dancers, to participate freely. This open-ended approach allows for a rich interplay of musical juxtaposition, creating a dynamic tapestry of sound that reflects our collective creativity and communal spirit.

Sammy in the Garden

Oil Pastels

Sammy with the Lizard in His Mouth

Oil Pastels

Nano Bites with Big Bucky Teeth

From the Nano Bites Collection

Part of the Sister*Soul Collection

Part of a larger art piece given to my dentist

He gave to his assistant

Love & Smile

Nano Bites

With Big Bucky Teeth Live

Part of a larger art piece

Live

More Nano Bites

Part of a larger Painting

Acrylic

One Nano Bite

Part of a larger Painting

Acrylic

Two Nano Bites

Part of a larger art piece called Nano Bites

(color inverted)

Acrylic

Nano Bites Swimming

Part of a larger art piece called Nano Bites

Acrylic

The Cosmic Egg

Water Color

The Cosmic Egg, the instant an idea, a thought becomes reality. It is the germ of all creation. This is a painting of an alien trying to steal the Cosmic Egg but instead steals an Easter egg. But, an Easter egg can also be thought of as rebirth, re-creation, as a sort of Cosmic Egg.

The Cosmic Egg

Etching & Collage

The Number 42 is significant. For those who have read "The Hitch Hikers Guide to the Galaxy" understand that when they fed the computer the question, "What is the meaning of life?" It spit out the number 42. The Cosmic Egg and the number 42 in this etching are the meaning of life and its significance. A just for fun etching.

ACRYLIC POUR PAINTINGS

Fish Jumping into the Sea

Acrylic Pour Painting

Red Sunflowers

Acrylic Pour Painting

Two Birds Wearing Hats

Acrylic Pour Painting

Two Birds & a Fish

Acrylic Pour Painting

Fishes Swimming

Acrylic Pour Painting

Dinosaurs

Acrylic Pour Painting

The Little Mermaid and her Friends
Seahorse, Tiger Fish, and Five AngelFish

"It was her love for her friends
the ocean, the coral
her friend
And the deep, deep Blues
And the Sea"

The Little Mermaid & Her Tiger Fish

Part of a larger painting

Acrylic on Canvas

The Little Mermaid & Her Tiger Fish

Study

MOSAIC GUITARS

Mosaic 12 String Guitar

(front)

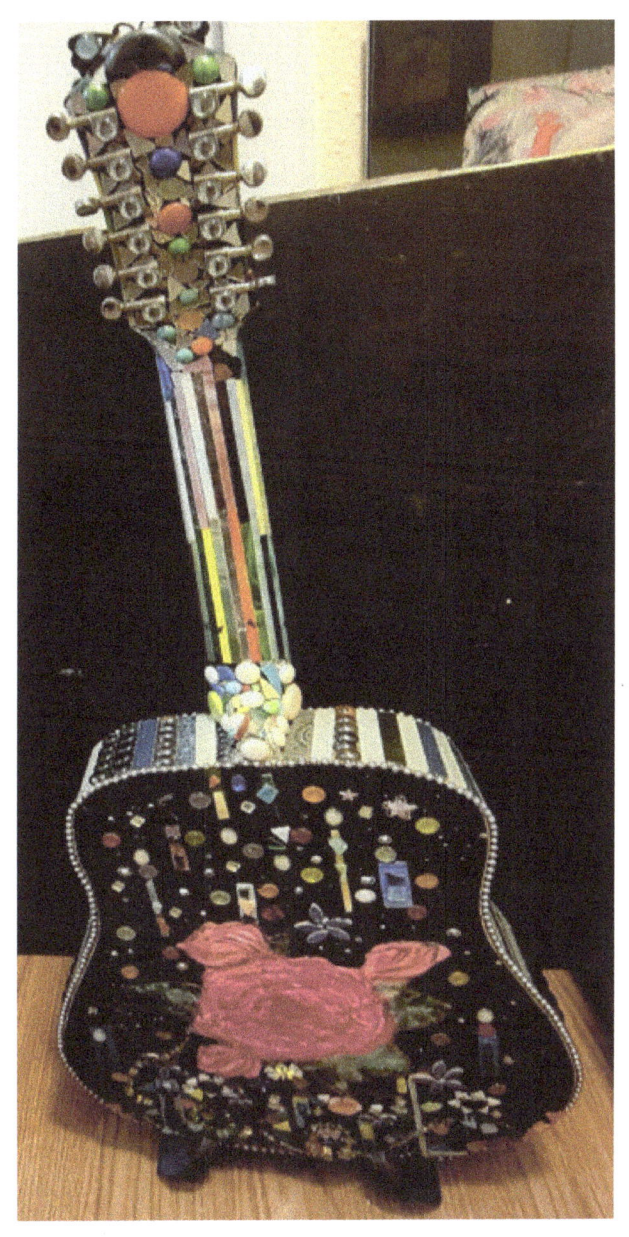

Mosaic 12 String Guitar

(back)

6 String Mosaic Guitar

(front)

6 String Mosaic Guitar

(back)

Mosaic Silverware Box

Found Art & Tiles

'I REMEMBER AS A YOUNG ADULT.

There's a scripture in the Bible that says, "All gifts come from God."

I am truly blessed and am eternally grateful. Niche, or was it Carl Sagan who wrote: "…that if you commit to the universe, the universe will commit to you."

Even though I was still very young, I remember saying out loud that

"I will commit to the universe,"

And I asked God to use me for good, use me as a vessel for creativity. Never do I want to use my hands for evil, for hurt, for sorrow.

And so it goes, my universe belongs to God, the Universe, to Love, Life and especially to creativity.

IN MY GARDEN
Part of "Sister*Soul" Pillow Cases

Flowers I

Part of a Pillowcase

Acrylic Paint

IN MY GARDEN IN MY GARDEN

In my garden, in my garden there is hope.

Hope that that keeps the sun's bounty

to shine through the darkest of days.

There is peace,

that no matter how much turmoil, no matter how much strife,

it is calm.

There is courage to do what's right and in victory

there is a quiet assurance that is my resolve.

I can believe in the world of color and of music.

I am a believer in the manifestations of the Universe's creation,

and I can embrace all things sacred.

In my garden, there is a belief

in the gentle courage of a whisper, inspired and is nurtured

And all the songs about life, about you,

about your whimsical smile,

the twinkle in your eyes

are now embedded in my heart. It all begins here

where flowers and even the weeds

smile back at me.

"All is Good."

Flowers II

Acrylic Alcohol Ink

Flowers III

Acrylic Alcohol Ink

Flowers IV

From "Sister*Soul" C0llection

Pillow Case

Acrylic Paint

"Time is nothing but a flash in the pan.
What was that?
A million years just leaped by."

Flowers V

From "In My Garden" Collection

"Gotta Keep Paying My Dues"

Dog Gone Prozac

Black Ink

Collage

DOG GONE PROZAC

& the Little BlueBird of Happiness

Happy as a Clam

Smoove Over

Dolphins Dance

While the Tookie Bird Watches

Over You & Me

JASPER

GRAPHITE

DOGS IS DOGS

Dogs is dogs
It's a wonderful thing
Don't leave them alone
Please give them a home
Hadn't anyone told you
Neglect is abuse
Mano to mano
There's no excuse
Neglect of course
It's a cryin' shame
Some folks kick them around
But he still your pal even to the end
Dogs is dogs
It's a family thing .
Here comes my dogs
Pookie Girl and Jasper, too,
Are you hungry today
Let's go out play,
Dog backwards is God, you know
What more can I say
My life's complete
With all of my dogs,
Bruiser, Biggie Bottom, and
Bear Puppy too

OUR BELOVED DOGS

Our Beloved Bruiser

acrylic & Collage

The Tail of Biggie Bottoms

Photo

Never did I imagine how such a marvelous entity could waltz into my life, into our lives. It was a day bathed in sunlight when Biggie arrived, a moment that felt almost magical. How could one little creature possess such purity of heart, soul, and essence? Biggie Bottoms emerged from the large box that held twelve puppies, his bright eyes sparkling with contagious delight. He strained with every ounce of his tiny being to cross over the lip of his enclosure. His spirit seemed boundless, and with unyielding determination, he leaped into our hearts, teaching us all the true meaning of love. As he bounded onto the floor, his excitement was so immense it felt like it could grow an entire forest. It was overwhelming in the most delightful way—a whirlwind of joy and energy. His tail wagged furiously, a vibrant flag of enthusiasm that never seemed to tire, nor did it ever want to slow down.

He's in my soul, in my heart,

He is my best friend.

Our Beloved Bruiser

'A song about our dogs'

"I'M THE KEEPER OF DOGS & CATS"

I'm the Keeper of Dogs & Cats

Sometimes I think I likes it like that

Yodel- le- he Yodel-le-he who

Oh, the Bruiser, he is my dog

He makes me feel ten feet tall

Yodel-le-he, Yodel-le-he who

Yodel-le-he who Yodel-le-he who

Yodel-le-he, Yodel-le-he who

Yodel-le-he who, Yodel-le-he who

Yodel-le-he, Yodel-le-he, Yodel-le-he, Yodel-le-he,

Yodel-le-he, Yodel-le-he, who

(cont.)

Pookie Girl

The Momacita Chula Linda

Photo

"I'M THE KEEPER OF DOGS & CATS"(CONT.)

Biggie Bottoms he likes to play

When I say go

He just stays

Yodel-le-he Yodel-le-he, who

Our Royal Flush

Right to Left

Pookie Girl, Bruiser, Jasper, Biggie Bottoms, and Bear Puppy

"I'M THE KEEPER OF DOGS & CAT" (CONT.)

He's the cat's meow

He's the doggies bow wow

He's the slow in the snail

The wag on the tail

He's Winnie the Pooh

Duke Ellington too

A Southern Gent

A Gentleman's Prince sent

Sugar Bear Ellington, aka Bear Puppy

photo

"I'M THE KEEPER OF DOGS & CATS" (CONT.)

God bless the little creatures of the earth & sea

God bless Mom & Pop

And you & me

(repeat mantra)

Brothers

Biggie Bottoms & Jasper

"I'M THE KEEPER OF DOGS & CATS"

I'm the Keeper of Dogs & Cats

Sometimes I think I likes it like that

Yo-del-le-he, Yo-del-le-he- who.

Ethos

A page from one of my Journals

"The way music makes us feel when we listen.

"Ethos is a Greek word meaning 'character' that is used to describe the guiding beliefs or ideals that characterize a community, nation or ideology, and the balance between caution and passion."

- Wikipedia

Dove in the Garden

Acrylic Alcohol Ink

Nope its very hard to admit
   That I do not like being disable
   I do not like it
      Not one bit.
         cclngsten 2023

Last but not least, I almost forgot about my cats, Popeye LePue' and Joey JoJo. They are not our pets. They are our children.

POPEYE LEPUE'

Popeye vacuming

When I first spotted Popeye, he was perched outside my window. For some time, I had been feeding and caring for the feral cats in my neighborhood as a devoted member of the San Antonio Feral Cat Society. They would drop off traps for me to catch the cats; once trapped, they would pick them up to have them spayed or neutered, then return them to my care, making me responsible for each and every one. That week, I had started feeding Popeye's three siblings, and by the end of the week, my gaze fell upon a new sight—Popeye himself. He was noticeably smaller than his brothers and sister, a delicate little creature all on his own.

It was early in the morning when I first laid eyes on Popeye. I knew immediately that he couldn't be his twin; his siblings had grown so much bigger in comparison. Driven by curiosity, I stepped outside to investigate this new little kitty, and I fell in love instantly. He was so small, so fragile, and I couldn't help but notice that his right eye was red and swollen while his left eye was also infected. Despite his ailments, he was feisty, standing on his back legs with his forearms raised, looking as though he were boxing. I gently picked him up and gave him a long, warm bath—something I think he truly enjoyed. After feeding him, he curled up between my arms and slept soundly through the night. The following morning, we took him to the veterinarian for a checkup.

We named him Popeye, inspired by the condition of his eye, which bore a striking resemblance to that of Popeye the Sailor Man. Despite his struggles, he was bursting with energy and life, a testament to his resilient spirit. It was heartbreaking to think about who or what had hurt him and damaged his eyes. He must have endured pain for about a week, hiding beneath the house until he finally gathered the courage to venture out. I affectionately nicknamed him Popeye LePue because he quickly became a little terror to all the cats, especially the females. Even in play, he exuded a mischievous energy that seemed to intimidate everyone, including me. My love for him is boundless; he is now Jay's big boy, and wherever Jay goes, Popeye follows closely, walking right between his feet. My love for my Popeye LePue is eternal."

JOEY JOJO

Joey JoJo was one of the feral cats I cared for at our home on Waverly Street, affectionately referred to as "the white house." We weren't evicted; rather, after the heavy snow and rains in San Antonio, the foundation of our beloved home was damaged. Although they repaired the foundation, the walls inside had opened up so much that you could literally look up through the ceiling and see the attic. Despite this upheaval, we received a glowing recommendation, and we proudly lived up to our reputation. JOJO's mother would frequently visit the side of the house for food, and I remember thinking how young she was, preparing to have her litter. That very week, she gave birth to four adorable kittens next door. When I began feeding the cats in my backyard, "Little Momita" brought her kittens to me, seeking a chance for them to thrive. She was incredibly smart, and I grew to love her dearly. Eventually, I started inviting them into the kitchen for feeding, and over time, they learned to trust me, allowing me to hold them. When I cradled JOJO in my arms, he would look up at me with curiosity, though I could sense a hint of mistrust lingering in his eyes. JOJO was both rambunctious and playful yet still very much feral. Nevertheless, he permitted me to shower him with love. I knew Popeye was coming with us, but I couldn't shake the desire to take JOJO, too. Initially, he was quite apprehensive about leaving his family behind. It took several months for him to truly feel at home in our new place. I simply couldn't leave him there to fend for himself; he was so small and naïve to the dangers of the outside world, especially cars. What a wonderful little kitty cat he is, and my heart is forever his to toy with. I suppose you could say I'm his "slave." As I often remind myself, "They are not just our pets; they are our children."

I've recorded and produced several CDs and Vinyl.

I've collaborated on CDs with Jay Fort's ensemble, "Nuclear Hamsters," and produced other albums, such as "Labor of Love," a compilation showcasing my music performed by talented musicians from Houston, Austin, and San Antonio. Additionally, I created "Falling," a tribute to the heroes, victims, and first responders of 9/11. My work also includes "Hamsters Or Us," which features Jay Fort's compositions, including "Rain Forest Lament." These recordings are available on platforms like CDBaby.com, YouTube, and Spotify, reaching listeners far and wide.

Currently, Jay and I finished recording our latest CD/Vinyl, *"Barely Legal,"* dedicated to DACA, the Dreamers, and also our concerns with what is happening at the border: that immigrants seeking asylum will never be treated as criminal, "We can all dream that all citizens of this blue and green planet are never treated as illegal and that the cruel and unjust legacy of "Operation Lone Star" will never be heard of again." When I saw this on the news, I was horrified to witness how Abbott allowed his Border Patrol agents to physically push back anyone attempting to climb out of the Rio Grande onto dry land. One particularly disturbing image showed an agent kicking a mother and her child, forcing them back into the water. It was heartbreaking. Why? "Porque es Mi Gente," "Because these are my people." This sentiment drives my passion and commitment to advocating for justice and compassion.

My music has always been a heartfelt expression, rooted in a dedicated belief in respecting my heritage, nurturing a love for humanity, upholding the Constitution, and cherishing this precious ideal we call democracy. Each note I play, and every lyric I write reflects my commitment to these values and the hope for a better world.

"The best thing for sadness is to learn."

- Merlin, from Camelot

ACTION MAGAZINE 1983

The Jazz Fusion of Carol Cisneros

Reônvó Menñes

Action Magazine, February 1983 • 9 •

Mark Hess (piano) & George Poole

219

JAY FORT'S NUCLEAR HAMSTERS

The Nuclear Hamsters excitingly explore the symbiotic relationship between modern jazz, human rights and global healing. Incorporating big band power with be-bop freedom, their music entices the listener to share the passion of artists who believe in world peace and environmental sustainability. Forcefully cosmic, but void of commercial exploitation, the Hamsters leave us with a clearer understanding of how music can create a positive new world mindset, enlightening the listener and expanding the realm of political jazz. A must for the intelligent music lover.

Rocky Boschert
KSYM-FM
San Antonio, Texas

"The Nuclear Hamsters excitingly explores the symbiotic relationship between modern jazz, human rights, and global healing. Incorporating big band power with be-bop freedom, their music entices the listener freedom, their music entices the listener to share their passion for artists who believe in world peace and environmental sustainability. Forcefully cosmic but void of commercial exploitation, the Hamsters leave us with a clearer understanding of how music can create a positive new world mindset, enlightening the listener and expanding the realm of political jazz. A must for the intelligent music lover.'

Rocky Boschert

KSYM-FM SA, TX

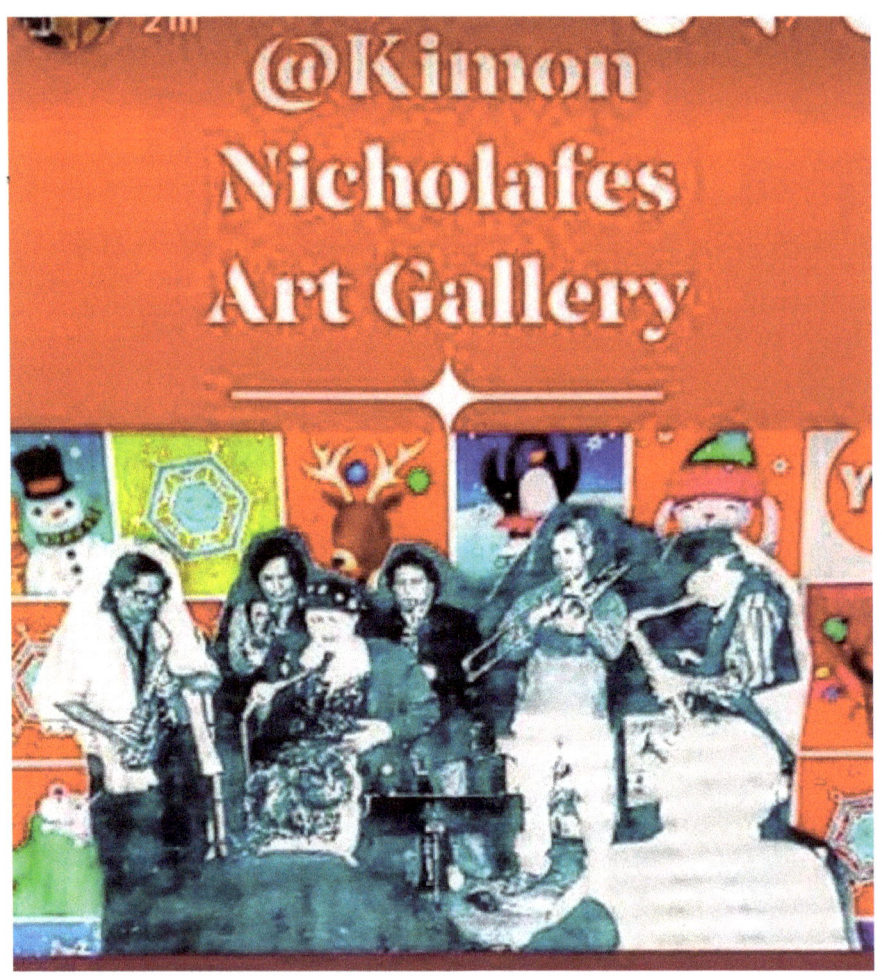

1998

Had to include this picture when we performed at Kimom Nicholaides Art Gallery. It was a very exciting gig. I also shared my art, and we had one big party, a BBQ. What was more exciting was that there was a huge storm outside, in fact, tornado weather. Joe Black was in charge of the BBQ as he stood between the outside and the gallery's back entrance. Somehow, we were too wonderful. These musicians were incredible.

Jay Fort - saxophone, to your left, Al Gomez - trumpet, Myself, Louis Bustos - alto saxophone. Armin Marmolejo - trombone, and Rocky Morales - Tenor sax.

"God, I love Jazz musicians."

2020

"We aim to please"

Jay Fort's NUclear*HAMsters

Jay Fort's Nuclear Hamsters, a contemporary jazz band, was born in Denton, Texas, in 1982, during Jay's time at North Texas State University. Now residing in San Antonio, Texas, Jay has continued to cultivate this vibrant musical project. The music we create draws from a diverse range of styles and experiences, conceived to be introspective yet danceable. It's full-blown jazz party music, infused with a serious vein of jazz to satisfy even the most discerning listeners. Originally, the brand name "Nuclear Hamsters" was created by Jay and his colleagues. He did a copyright of the logo.

The 'Nuclear Hamsters, ' the idea of the band's name and the mushroom cloud logo, was a reaction to a threat of Nuclear War and sad the state of affairs happening at that time of early 1980's.

During my time as a student at SWT, I heard that another group in Denton had also adopted the name "Nuclear Hamsters." I remember responding with a hopeful, "Hope they're good!" To make our identity clearer and more personal, I later added 'Jay Fort's' to the name, making it uniquely ours.

When Jay and I met, he told me about the group. I thought to myself, "Way too cool!" and immediately, I wanted to be a 'Nuclear Hamster."

We embarked on a musical journey, and together, we performed, laughed, channeled our love of humanity, our dogs, our planet, and also our democracy. Our musicians whose extremely powerful musicianship, and some who have stayed with us, it seems like forever. I am immensely grateful to Al Gomez, one of the most talented trumpet players in San Antonio—and, indeed, the world. Currently, he is touring with Jimmy Vaughn, a testament to his incredible skill. We also honor the contributions of George Prado, Brandon Rivas, Jorge Palomo, and Pete Ojeda, our beloved bass players who are with us in spirit. What can I say? I feel truly blessed that they all love playing with us. Our rhythm section includes Chuck Glave, Kevin Hess, and Armando "Mando" Ausenat on drums, along with Eric Castillas on percussion. I would also like to give a special shout-out to "Blue Cat Recording Studio" and my favorite producer and engineer, Joe Trevino, as well as "Mauro," a brilliant and magical engineer who consistently makes our music sound incredible. My gratitude for all of them is boundless; I am eternally thankful.

One of our latest CDs/Vinyl is entitled "Barely Legal." A dedication to DACA, the Dreamers, and also our concerns with what is happening at the border. We can all dream that one day, all citizens of this world will never be treated as illegal and that the cruel and unjust legacy of "Operation Lone Star" will never be heard of again. "Porque es Mi Gente." Because these are my people.

My grandmother was an immigrant from Mexico who bravely fled during the Mexican Revolution, escaping the brutal and oppressive tyranny of Santa Anna. Her journey is a testament to resilience and courage, and it shapes my understanding of the struggles that many face in pursuit of a better life.

And so, here I am, joyfully singing and swinging with Jay Fort's Nuclear Hamsters, embracing every moment of this incredible musical journey.

Oh, Happy Day!

"Barely Legal"

(a suite)

dedicated to DACA, the Dreamers.

UPC/EAN

198026131331

"Barely Legal"

The Musicians

Back of Vinyl

The Rain Forest Lament

UPC/EAN

194171752995

A Labor of Love

UPC/EAN

190394373023

Falling

UPC/EAN

19417174253

Hamsters Or Us

Jay Fort's Nuclear Hamsters

UPC/EAN

191924019992

NOT
The End

"Only the beginning of another chapter in my life."

"Barely Legal" CD

UPC/EAN (codes)

1. "Barely Legal" - 198026131331

ISRC - QMAAK2362140

2. "Sangre' de Mis Hermanos de Alma"

ISRC - QMAAK2362141

3. "SA Chillin'"

ISRC - QMAAK2362142

4. "Csi's Blues"

ISRC - QMAAK2362143

5. "Wednesday Blues"

ISRC - QMAAK2362144

6. "Los Pinche' Bean Jam Blues"

ISRC - QMAAK2362145

"Rain Forest Lament" CD

UPC/EAN

- 1941171752995

1. Rain Forest Lament with Jazz Chamber Ensemble

IRSC - usl4q1938374

2. "Ballad Borsht"

IRSC - usl4q1938375

3. "Rev. Falala" Big Band

IRSC - usl4q1938376

4. "Listen to the Wind"

IRSC - usl4q1938377

5. "Gotta' Keep Paying My Dues"

IRSC - usl4q1938378

6. "Rain Forest Lament " electronic soundscape

IRSC - usl4q1938379

Falling" CD

" UPC/EAN

19417174253

1. "Falling"ssss

ISRC - ushm91903586

2. "I'm the Keeper of Dogs & cats"

IRSC - ushm91903587

3. "Blues Monday"

IRSC - 91903588

4. "The Singer"

IRSC - ushm91903589

5. "Donna's World Peace & Unity Song" (a Soldier's Lament)

IRSC - ushm91903590

"Labor of Love" CD

UPC/EAN - 190394373023

1. "Labor of Love"

ISRC- uscgj16380603

2. "Chrysalis"

ISRC - uscgj1638060

3. "I'm the Keeper of Dogs & Cats"

ISRC - uscgj1638061

4. "Womanizer"

ISRC - uscgj1638062

5. "Don't Let It Get You Down"

ISRC - uscgj1638064

THE BLOG

Ms. Cisneros encapsulates a remarkable journey filled with both triumphs and tribulations, showcasing her unwavering dedication to personal growth and creative endeavors. She speaks candidly about her life, sharing her experiences with an openness that invites connection. Despite living with disabilities and chronic pain for most of her life, she has embraced her identity as a musician, fine artist, poet, and a passionate believer in humanity, all while nurturing her love for this blue and green planet we call home.

Within her work, she shares a rich tapestry of art, music compositions, poems, and writings that reflect her vibrant spirit. One of her standout pieces, "Not One Bit," is a poem inspired by her favorite childhood author, Dr. Seuss. In it, she candidly addresses her disabilities while expressing her aspirations to fly, soar, and dance freely—perhaps even have a fit if she so chooses. Her words resonate with passion and determination, revealing her compulsion to create, whether through music compositions, songs, poetry, or visual art.

Moreover, Ms. Cisneros is a beacon of encouragement for those grappling with mental, physical, and spiritual pain. She urges everyone to discover and pursue their passions, reminding us that such pursuits can be a source of healing and fulfillment. As an educator, she feels a profound responsibility to inspire others to learn as much as they can. She believes that the ability to learn is one of the greatest gifts bestowed upon humanity by God or the universe, and she emphasizes that there is so much to explore. Whether it's learning to play the guitar, piano, or any instrument, writing down one's deepest and most intimate thoughts, or expressing creativity through painting or drawing, she encourages everyone to embrace their imagination. You never know what wonderful creations may arise from the depths of your creativity.

About the Author

Carol Cisneros M.M., Fine Artist, Advanced Printmaking, Master Music Composition/Performance, Guitarist, Piano, Jazz Vocalist, Poet, Humanitarian, and Nature lover, especially animals and the forest.

An accomplished guitarist, pianist, jazz vocalist, composer, educator, producer, author, fine artist, and graphic designer.

I was five years old when I started to play piano. I stayed with my grandmother Cisneros, where there was an upright piano. At that time, my father couldn't afford piano lessons, but I wanted to learn to play so bad that I taught myself to read the children's piano books that were in the piano bench. The ones with the little elf and animals they were my guides. I understood where the middle "C" was located on the keyboard, where my fingers were placed on the keyboard.